CW00833501

R. B. HALL

AND

HIS BANDS

a Biography by
Gordon W. Bowie, Ph. D.

TABLE OF CONTENTS

PREFACE AND ACKNOWLEDGEMENTS

This project would have been impossible without the contributions of a great many people over the last fifteen years, and I would like to express my gratitude.

The need for a study such as this first came to my attention during a time about 1980, when the idea of R. B. Hall Day was first being seriously discussed. The late Bangor physician James D. Clement, Jr., who played tuba in the Bangor Band, was in the process of collecting and assembling parts to Hall's out-of-print marches. He was collaborating with band historian and Hall biographer Thomas C. Bardwell, Sr., to create reissues of the *R. B. Hall Superior Band Book*, Mace Gay's collection of *Hall's Marches*, and the *R. B. Hall and the State of Maine*

band book. All three had long been out of print and unavailable. Through the efforts of these two men, and the others who helped them, the majority of Hall's marches that had passed out of publication and faded into obscurity were once again made more widely available.

Under the directorship of the late University of Maine Associate Professor Robert C. Collins, the Bangor Band was playing many of these newly rediscovered marches, and interest in Hall was being maintained. Under Collins, who died in 1983, I was able to play most of the marches from the Superior and Mace Gay books, and thus gain an appreciation of many more of Hall's marches than

those in the Fischer books which had been commonly available prior to that time.

In 1982, Dr. Clement asked me to expand the arrangement of Hall's march *Kineo*, for which he had only seven original parts, so that it could be played by a present-day band and could be included in the *State of Maine* book he was assembling at the time. That project marked the beginning of my serious interest in bringing Hall's out of print compositions up to date. Dr. Clement was indefatigable in his efforts to collect all of Hall's music, as well as that of other Maine composers, for the Bangor Band. By the time he died in 1988 he had collected and together with Bardwell reprinted almost all of Hall's output for band.

The informational base for this project was largely the result of the efforts of Thomas C. Bardwell, Sr., who collected and assembled the *R. B. Hall Anthology* of band tape recordings, and who in 1990 donated his entire collection of Hall material to the University of Maine. Bardwell had long been active in sending tapes of Hall's marches to other bandsmen and band directors; much of the material he sent to Dr. Clement, Prof. Collins, and Bangor Band President Samuel D. Wyman, Jr., was also shared with me. Later, when I became conductor of the Bangor Band once again, I began to receive tapes directly from Bardwell, whom I came to know much better after the 1988 R. B. Hall Day in Bridgton, Maine.

Special thanks are due to Robert Hudson, conductor of the Augusta Civic Symphony Orchestra and its associated community band, who gave me his entire file of correspondence pertaining to Hall research and the creation of R.B. Hall Day at the time he moved out of Maine.

Throughout this entire project I have had the friendship, encouragement, and support of Samuel D. Wyman. Jr., president of the Bangor Band and its tuba player. "Sam" has given me many valuable pieces of band history such as clippings, pamphlets, programs and scrapbooks, and helped me find elusive music, such as parts to Hall's *March 6/8*. He

has shared band tapes and correspondence that have been of immense value. As an informant in the Bangor Band history project, he has made taped interviews with me, and also shared his long knowledge of band history informally.

Special thanks should go to Ralph Gould for his taped interview and loan of many interesting items of ephemera. Also to Bangor Band members Leo C. Thayer, Jr., Hal Wheeler, and the late Sam Viner, all of whom were informants for the oral history portion of the project. Also to Bangor Band members Daniel Priestly and Harris Southard for the loan of hard to find books.

The entire Bangor Band has contributed greatly to this study, both individually and collectively, as we have rehearsed and performed so many of Hall's less-well-known pieces. They have also contributed by their tolerance for my preoccupation with writing during these last few months.

I would like to thank the members of my Doctoral Committee for their time, effort, and friendship. At the very outset when I "sort of had an idea for a book," I inquired of University of Maine Professor Richard M. Jacobs, Bangor Symphony Principal Clarinet, Stammtisch Band clarinet player and friend, on a summer Sunday outing, about the possibility of "involving the University." He sug-

gested that I consider enrolling for further graduate study, and so began the process that has led to this dissertation.

Chairman of the committee, Professor Edward D. (Sandy) Ives, has given me encouragement, advice, and the voice of experience in our frequent meetings throughout the entire writing process. Professors James Acheson and Stanley S. Pliskoff have given much time in advice, encouragement and tutelage. University of Connecticut Professor David M. Maker has given much insight and advice from afar. In spite of the distance he is very much a part of this project.

Librarians have been very important to the research phase of this dissertation. It was through the efforts of Director of Libraries and Professor Elaine M. Albright that the acquisition of the Bardwell collection, so important to this study, was made possible. I would especially like to thank Special Collections Librarian Muriel Sanford of Raymond Fogler Library at the University of Maine; Acquisitions and Special Collections Librarian P. A. Lynn at Colby College; and Jon Newsome and Wilda Heiss at the Music division of the Library of Congress.

Master Chief Musician Bob Gloff at the United States Navy Band Library, and Master Gunnery Sergeant Mike Ressler at the United States Marine Band Library, were both most helpful in the matter of looking for and examining the parts to unusual Hall titles. Often these turned out to be composed by someone other than R. B. Hall. The kindness of friend and amateur trombonist Dr. E. Donald Blodgett of the United States Department of Education facilitated my research visit to Washington, D. C., where he opened for me many doors that would have been otherwise inaccessible.

Finally, I would like to thank my wife, Mary, who has supported and encouraged this project from the very beginning. She has been an invaluable assistant in so many phases of the study, but especially in managing the computer system and teaching me to use it, in preparing the computer graphics, and in the final editing and assembly process.

—Gordon W. Bowie, May 1993

ABOUT THIS EDITION

JUNE 2007

What follows is an excerpt of the biographical portions of the dissertation, completed in 1993, that resulted in the awarding of my doctoral degree. In the intervening years there has been much interest among bandsmen and others in Hall's biography, and many requests for me to make available a shorter version of the original thesis, which totaled more than 450 pages. In doing so I have had to leave out much fascinating material on the history of bands in Maine, and community bands in general, and the musical analysis of many of Hall's marches. The reader who wishes to read the complete work can order my dissertation, *R. B. Hall and the Community Bands of Maine*, from U. M. I., 300 N. Zeeb Road, Ann Arbor, MI 48106. The order number is 9325868. Any university or public library can assist in this ordering process.

This edition is being published in honor of the 100th anniversary of R. B. Hall's death.

INTRODUCTION: THE GOLDEN AGE OF BAND MUSIC

The golden age of band music in America began in the last part of the nineteenth century and continued through the first decade and a half of the twentieth century. The mechanisms of brass and woodwind instruments had developed sufficiently by then, so that their mastery was possible by people of ordinary talent, and mass production combined with commercial distribution had brought them within affordability for an increasing number of Americans. Even for the ordinary person, affluence and leisure time were increasing in the tide of post-civil-war industrial prosperity. People wanted entertainment, people wanted activity, people wanted music, and band music was perfectly suited to the popular needs.

Every kind of public gathering was improved by the addition of band music. Parades, civic occasions, picnics, and outings all required music. Political campaigns and electioneering, with their customary torchlight processions, needed loud, portable music. Evening serenades were a popular way of charming a sweetheart, or toasting a popular personage. Band concerts on the town square became a favorite pastime in every community fortunate enough to have a band. Town bands, community and civic bands, military bands, lodge and fraternal bands, and professional bands proliferated in response to the demand. Band music remained popular as a predominant form of public musical entertainment until after the First World War, when changing economic and social conditions, together with the advent of electromechanically reproduced music, signaled its decline.

Such a proliferation of bands necessitated new music for them to play, and although some of the bigger and later bands performed transcriptions from orchestral classics, public tastes favored more accessible forms. Marches, quicksteps, waltzes, polkas, schottisches, and patriotic potpourris were favored. Virtuoso solos, favorite tunes from popular operas, and medleys of tin-pan-alley favorites became staples of the band repertoire. Of all this music, however, the form which became most strongly identified with the band was the march. Marches were played not only for parades and processions, but also for dancing. Bands needed marches to play: bandmasters and composers filled the bill with an enormous output, most of which is by now forgotten. A few bandmasters who were also march writers became famous enough so that their work remained in the repertoire. The most well-known of their marches are still widely played by bands today.

The most famous of these bandmaster-composers was John Philip Sousa (1854-1932), whose name became a household word following his successful world tours. His reputation was enhanced by the publicity surrounding both his life and his career which took him to the show-business centers of America and the world. Sousa's phenomenal success began with an early start in the United States Marine Band. It continued with a timely move to show-business with entrepreneur David Blakeley, in a field vacated by the death of the leading bandmaster and showman of the day, Patrick Gilmore. Another forty years of ceaseless touring with a large fully-instrumented band left a veritable army of Sousa band alumni to carry his reputation forward. Finally, an enormous productive output that included not only his famous marches, but also operettas, waltzes, songs, novels, literary articles, letters to the editor, and voluminous correspondence ensured for Sousa the preeminent place his reputation enjoys among bandsmen to this day.

Many other bandmasters were well known in their time as composers in the march genre. An example is David Wallis Reeves (1838-1900), director of the American Band of Providence, Rhode Island, a voluminous composer whose many marches are often referred to by band scholars, but with the sole exception of his *2nd Connecticut N. G. March* seldom heard anymore. The great circus bandmasters, such as Russell Alexander (1877-1915) and Karl L. King (1891-1971), came later and many of their marches are still played to this day. Henry Fillmore (1881-1956) built an impressive reputation as a civic and fraternal band leader and radio showman, in addition to being a prolific composer and publisher. He composed well over a hundred marches under his own name and various pseudonyms; many of his marches are still favorites with band musicians and audiences alike.

The fact that most bandmasters of the era composed and arranged for their bands produced a number of well-known march writers in almost every region of the country. Willimantic, Connecticut produced Thomas H. Rollinson (1844-1928), who was an extremely prolific writer of marches as well as other musical forms. Pennsylvania bandmaster William Paris Chambers (1854-1913) composed many fine marches, cornet solos, and other pieces. A long list of others, many of whom lived and composed well into the twentieth century, includes local favorites in many states and several regions.

Unique in many respects is Maine composer and bandmaster Robert Browne Hall (1858-1907), who is known primarily by his marches. Many of these are well known to bandsmen in America, Europe, and England, where they are still frequently played. Hall's marches hold a place of respect, perhaps second only to those of Sousa.

Although Hall composed a large number of marches—once thought to be more than a hundred—and several musical pieces in other forms, and was well known as a cornet soloist and bandmaster during his lifetime, he lived a relatively private life for an entertainer. He left no writings other than his music. Unlike Sousa or Fillmore, there was no diary, ledger, or collections of letters to editors, not even a body of letters to friends or relatives. Concerned with the daily exigencies of his work, he did not seem to have a sense that his marches might have a future importance larger than his contemporary reputation. Consequently, his life-story has been a mystery to the generations of musicians who have revered his music but have known little of the man. Speculations and assumptions about the titles of some of his marches have given rise to some rather wild and apocryphal tales. The general paucity of readily available biographical detail has been a source of curiosity to many.

Questions abound: Who was Robert Browne Hall, the man? Why were his works so enduring and endearing? What is the significance of many of the titles of his marches, so many of which seem, elusively, to be related to some event, individual, or location of personal significance to Hall? What of his influence on the many bands with which he was associated? What legacy was carried forward by his pupils and the band musicians with whom he worked?

Unanswered questions such as these invite speculation and assumptions. For several generations, band musicians have been using their imaginations to fill in the details of Hall's life. Given a handful of march titles and a small, but constantly recirculated pool of sketchy biographical information, bandsmen have created a "legendary" R. B. Hall to fill their need for knowledge of the person who created these well-liked works.

The biography that follows is an attempt to assemble and reconcile all the known source stories and material concerning R. B. Hall's life and works. Considerable emphasis has been placed on newspaper accounts of Hall's concerts and doings. In an era when the activities of the town band and local musicians were important news, they give a good picture of his professional activities. Oral testimony and the recollections of Hall's last pupils are also important in reconstructing some of the events of his final years. In spite of the fact that information about Hall's personal life remains incomplete the tale of his life and doings is still a source of fascination.

CHAPTER ONE
HALL'S EARLY LIFE AND CAREER

Because of the low profile that Hall kept during most of his life, there is some confusion and uncertainty concerning his early career and student days. Little is known of his childhood except what has been reported by his sisters. Conflicting testimony and apocryphal tales concerning his first years in the band business abound, and the authors of the several short biographical sketches that have appeared over the years seem to differ on important details. For instance, military band historian William White wrote in 1944 that R.B. Hall was an E-flat cornet player, making no mention of him ever playing a B-flat cornet.[1] Most other sources, including Ralph Gould's 1967 *Down East* magazine article which is probably the most authoritative and detailed of the existing general biographical sketches, describe as him changing from the E-flat cornet to the B-flat cornet, and it is indeed a B-flat instrument with which Hall is usually pictured.[2]

Almost the only biographical information about which there have been no conflicting statements is that which is part of the official documentary record, that is birth, marriage, death. Robert Browne Hall was born on June 30, 1858, at Abbagadasset Point, Bowdoinham, Maine, in his mother's family home. His parents were Nathaniel W. Hall, of Nobleboro, a blacksmith by trade, and Virginia Lodoeska Browne Hall. He was married at the age of 43, on January 29, 1902, to Izzie Alta Luce, of Waterville, aged 19. He died on June 8, 1907 at his mother's home in Portland, of kidney disease. Those short facts are available at the Maine State Archives, in Augusta, Maine. What happened between those events has been the subject of numerous and conflicting tales.

Part of the problem has been the need for brevity when a newspaper wanted just a few words or a few inches on Hall's background: condensation can lead to distortion. Part has been the recirculation of material from the same few original sources, and an attempt by some writers to extrapolate and interpolate when facts are missing. In any event what we know of Hall's early life is dependent on just a few sources, and from their testimony a picture of the young musician emerges.

When R.B. Hall was still very young, his parents moved from Bowdoinham to Richmond, a larger village about five miles up the river from Abagadassett Point. Richmond was a thriving river town, with steamers leaving for Boston and Portland, and a railroad that brought passengers from inland points to board the boats there. Many large ships were built and launched from Richmond yards. After the Kennebec River bridge was built at Bath, Richmond's importance as a port quickly dwindled, and its economic role diminished as shipping became centered in Bath. During Hall's youth, however, Richmond was in its heyday of activity.

Beyond the bare fact of his birth, most of what was known of Hall's early years was gleaned from talks with his sisters, Mrs. Alice Hall Thurlow, of Richmond, and Miss Virginia Hall of Portland, who were contacted for journalistic pieces whenever interest in R. B. Hall's past was rekindled. They told of Hall's early interest in and natural ability for music. Walter Sturtevant, Richmond's self-appointed town historian, kept an extensive and detailed diary. Because he had been a musician in the town band during the years of Hall's youth, Sturtevant recorded many of the observations and anecdotes that now make up the history of Hall's early experiences. Unfortunately, the school in Richmond had

PLATE 1 R. B. HALL'S BIRTHPLACE ON ABAGADASSET POINT (Courtesy of Bagaduce Music Lending Library)

burned in 1928, and all official records of Hall's early years and schooling were lost.[3]

Both sides of Hall's family were musical. The Browne Family Orchestra was an accomplished string group, well-known throughout the Kennebec Valley. Virginia (R. B. Hall's mother) was an accomplished pianist, and proficient on the violin, lute, harp and classical guitar. Nathaniel (R. B. Hall's father) was a cornet player, earlier a regionally acclaimed keyed bugler, who founded the Richmond Band in 1854. Prior to that, he was E-flat cornet soloist and leader of the Nobleboro Silver Cornet Band.[4] He

PLATE 2 THE BROWNE FAMILY ORCHESTRA. L to R: Bainbridge, Georgia, Virginia (R.B.H.'s mother), Mary Bartlett, Robert, Edwin, America, Loyalist (Courtesy of Bagaduce Music Lending Library)

Hall's youth in Richmond. Among them was Walter Sturtevant, who had played cornet in the Richmond Cornet Band, and was the acknowledged town philosopher and historian. Acclaimed locally as a "literary genius," Sturtevant kept a daily diary, to which he referred while being interviewed by Bateman. Sturtevant was leader of the Richmond Cornet Band before Hall learned to play, and had taken over as leader again when Hall left for other engagements. As an old man in 1922 he still enjoyed playing his cornet.

Although much of the available biographical material suggests that Hall's father was his first teacher,[5] first-hand witnesses Alice Hall Thurlow, Herbert Mansir, and Walter Sturtevant all told Bateman otherwise. After his interview with Mrs. Thurlow, Bateman wrote: "From a child he was a musical genius, but was not encouraged by his father for an education along that line. Of a delicate physical constitution it was thought that a wind instrument like the cornet would be too severe for his lungs and therefore it was opposed by his father." Bateman quotes Walter Sturtevant as saying: "When the father was on his death bed he said: 'Don't let Bert play the cornet. He is too frail, and it will end in consumption as it has with me.'"[6]

In spite of this injunction against playing wind instruments, his sister reported: "Wherever and whenever he could get a

became ill in 1872 and died in 1874, when R. B. Hall was 16 years old.

A two-page feature in the June 15, 1922 issue of the *Lewiston Journal (fift*een years after Hall's death) gives what is probably the most complete extant review of Hall's early childhood and career. For this, writer Luther C. Bateman, who was publisher of the *Lewiston Journal,* and who had lived in Waterville during much of the time that Hall was active as a musician there, interviewed Alice Hall Thurlow and several other Richmond residents who had recollections of chance to play some instrument he always took advantage of the occasion to learn." [7] But it wasn't until 1874 that he started playing the cornet seriously. Mrs. Thurlow continued: "When but sixteen years of age he adopted the cornet as his choice and in a short time became an expert on that instrument." [8]

Herbert Mansir of Richmond, who had been listed by Sturtevant as a member of Hall's band, poured out the complete story in Bateman's article. "When Bert Hall began his musical career in this village I gave him his first lessons on the cornet. It was but a short time, however, before I was taking lessons from him!"

Hall's next teacher was Newell Perkins of Lewiston, a cornetist of considerable local fame, who preferred the B-flat cornet over the E-flat. Perkins was to become leader of the Auburn Cadet Band, and co-leader of Glover's Band (in which George Glover played E-flat, and Perkins the B-flat cornet) and eventually went west to found an excellent band in Boise City, Idaho.[9] According to Ralph Gould, Hall commuted from Bowdoinham to Lewiston for these lessons, and it was while under Perkins' tutelage that he switched from E-flat to B-flat cornet.[10] According to Alice Hall Thurlow this lesson arrangement lasted only for a single year, 1875. He may have had some casual instruction from cornetist W. W. Brown, leader of the

Bowdoinham band, and a friend of Hall's who later frequently played with Hall's band, not as a regular member, but just to help out when needed.[11]

The issue of whether and when Hall switched from E-flat to B-flat cornet is important because the choice of his main instrument defined Hall's generational relationship to the music around him and the music he ultimately created. Nathaniel Hall (R. B. Hall's father) had played keyed bugle, and later E-flat cornet. That was appropriate for a musician of his era, but changing times would require a different approach.

During the 1850s keyed and valved brasses were played side by side, but by the time of the Civil War, as volunteer militia bands enlisted and regular army bands were supplied with instruments, valved instruments had completely supplanted their keyed progenitors. The E-flat cornet was the logical successor to the soprano keyed bugle (also pitched in E-flat). The keyed bugle had been invented in England about 1810, and was introduced to America about 1815.[12] It was the solo voice of brass bands from the early nineteenth century until about 1860 when the valved cornet, invented in Europe around 1820, had spread in use and gradually become accepted in America as the superior and more modern instrument. The famed musical duel between Patrick Gilmore's E-

flat cornet and Ned Kendall's E-flat keyed bugle, on a rendition of John Holloway's *Wood Up Quick Step,* took place in Salem, Massachusetts, in 1856.[13] It proved beyond a doubt the superiority of the more modern instrument.

The E-flat pitch was still regarded as the solo soprano voice, however, and the E-flat soprano cornet, about forty inches long, was not completely displaced by its larger (55-inch) B-flat relative until the turn of the century. During the 1860s the B-flat was considered an alto to the E-flat's soprano. After the Civil War, the B-flat instrument gradually came to replace the E-flat as the leading voice of the brass section.[14] Sturtevant's band list of the Richmond Cornet Band from about 1875 listed R. B. Hall as an E-flat cornet.[15]

What is important is that if Hall had written his marches for an E-flat lead voice, they would not have retained their popularity into the twentieth century. No matter how tuneful, they would have been relegated to the status of antiques had they not been playable by a modern band. Since they were conceived for a B-flat cornet as the lead voice they immediately became "modern," and they have survived, unlike many others written by Hall's predecessors.

This has been the fate of most of the marches composed in the decade or two prior to Hall's emergence as a composer. For example, of the hundred or so outstanding marches composed by the legendary David Wallis Reeves (1838-1900) only one (the *Second Regiment Connecticut N. G. March*) is remembered today. The same could be said for pre-Civil War bandmaster Claudio S. Grafulla (1810-1880) whose only remembered march was the *Washington Grays*. This had been arranged by Louis Laurendau[16] to be playable with the B-flat lead, but even so it is considered extremely difficult. Recently several other Grafulla works from the *Port Royal Band Books*, written (all in manuscript, of course) while his Third New Hampshire Regiment Band was in Port Royal (near Charleston, South Carolina) during the Civil War, have been re-instrumented by present-day arrangers. These are now playable with modern instrumentation, and Grafulla's reputation is having a resurgence. In contrast, R. B. Hall conceived his pieces with the B-flat cornet as the lead voice in his mind, and that is one major reason why they have found such ready acceptance among bandsmen from that day to this.

Walter Sturtevant was Richmond's town philosopher and *de facto* town historian. He had kept a journal through the entire era while Hall was growing up and becoming involved in Richmond's bands. Later his diaries were to become the basis for John Daly Fleming's book, *Richmond on the Kennebec*.[17] Sturtevant was Bateman's source for some of the most important anecdotes about Hall's youthful years. One important anecdote deals with Hall's lameness, and the fact that he occasionally used a crutch, but would do without it if it was thought to detract from the effect of his performance. As told by Sturtevant, the following anecdote would have taken place when Hall was 18 years old.

Bert Hall was the soul of good humor and fun, while his fearlessness was proverbial. In 1876 he went to Old Orchard against the protest of all his friends. At the time I was a telegraph operator in the depot and when he came to get his ticket he was on a crutch, having some serious trouble. He was advised not to go as people would not relish seeing a cornet player on crutches. Hall immediately handed his crutch to me and boarded the train as tho nothing was wrong. It was a marvelous example of fortitude and pluck, as he must have been in severe pain at the time. [18]

Sturtevant's narrative details the rivalry between the Richmond Band (begun by Hall's father, Nathaniel Hall, in 1854) and the Richmond Cornet Band, which came into existence about 1873, and of which Sturtevant was for a time the leader. As Sturtevant told

PLATE 3. R. B. HALL AS A YOUNG MAN (About 1876, Age 18). (Courtesy of Bagaduce Music Lending Library)

Bateman: "Then Hall led here for a time and then started Hall's band, and it was a success from the start. This was about the year 1878." Eventually, what remained of the Richmond Cornet Band was known as Hall's Band.

After the Richmond Band left to go on a tour around the world on General Grant's flagship, about 1879, those who didn't go joined Hall's Band. According to Sturtevant: "In the meantime Hall was gone a great deal, playing in Bangor, Waterville, Albany, and other places, but the band kept on giving outdoor concerts, and playing in other places as well as Richmond." [19]

Could this have been the secret to the legendary proliferation of Hall's multiple early successes, that he trained the Richmond Cornet Band, and then left for other engagements, while the band played on without him? The Richmond Cornet Band (Hall's Band) collapsed in the winter of 1882, coinciding with the time that Hall left Richmond permanently.

One other story that emphasizes Hall's lameness stems from this era in the days when he was leading the Richmond Cornet Band. It has been told and retold in many of the retrospectives, and concerns an evening excursion to a party down the Kennebec River from Richmond that the band played on a barge "propelled by two sculling oars and the tide." After the evening's festivities were over, the boat docked at the town landing, and Hall was left behind. In Mildred Beedle Fossett's words:

When it was time to start for home the young people paired up and the ferry boat slowly crawled back to Richmond. As the couples left the boat at the Town Landing, it was the intention of each swain to escort his young lady home. So intent were they on this procedure that they completely forgot that their leader, who had a physical infirmity of lameness, required their assistance.

Hall was left, alone and deserted, and considerable time passed before some of the boys on their way home (after having bid their ladies good night) discovered their abandoned leader. They apologetically helped him home as he laughingly told them that he had begun to wonder when he and "home, sweet home" were to be united. He never laid it up against them, and in after years whenever the incident was mentioned he always produced a hearty laugh as he recalled the time he spent in the "wee, small hours" of a morning waiting at the wharf. [20]

Herbert Mansir, who played the E-flat bass in the Richmond band, was an informant for both L. C. Bateman and Mildred Beedle Fossett. Like many brass bandsmen of the day Mansir played a little on all the instruments. These instruments all had a similar technique, but differed mainly in size and required agility, which gave them different roles in the instrumentation. Involved in the Richmond band all his life, he was voluble in his appreciation of Hall. Mansir had been Hall's first teacher on the cornet.

Mansir had played in Hall's bands in Richmond through the later 1870s, and continued to play long after Hall left Richmond for the greater world. He told Bateman of Hall's style with his bands, giving later generations an insight into what it was that made Hall's bands so outstanding:

I played in his band and he was always the same, although strict in his discipline. He trained the members and made them work. That is the reason Hall's Band enjoyed a reputation second to none other in all New England. Had it not been for that he would never have been called to Bangor, Waterville. Boston, and Albany. [21]

Hall's Richmond Band posed for a group photograph on Richmond's main street in March of 1878. This was about the time that they took a pledge to abstain from alcoholic beverages at performances.

It is interesting to note that on December 10, 1877, the members of the Richmond Cornet Band signed a solemn pact that they would abstain from all intoxicating liquor "at such times and places as the Band may be called upon to do duty." [22]

PLATE 4. HALL'S BAND IN RICHMOND. Taken on Main Street, 1878. R. B. Hall appears in the forward center holding an E-flat cornet. (Courtesy of Bagaduce Music Lending Library)

Sturtevant's tale of the Richmond and Hall's bands continues:

Then came a hiatus, as it were. At a business meeting it was voted to suspend further work until due notice. But Hall's Band could not die and the next Memorial day we again got together and played. July 7th, 1880 Hall returned and the band began to revive and that year we played at many rallies and concerts. Hall was no longer a well man, but he continued to work beyond his strength. In the winter of 1881 and 1882 Hall left and I was again

leader of the band. We continued for another year before the band was broken up.[23]

It is interesting that Hall's health was already an issue at the age of 22. It had been as issue as he was growing up, and he was to continue to be plagued by poor health off and on throughout his life. Lameness is the primary difficulty that is mentioned by most sources, though no one ever said to what condition it was attributable. Whatever its cause, it was an obstacle to his marching, but he marched in spite of it, often with his cane hung over his arm as he played.

Hall also had continuing respiratory difficulties, often necessitating a convalescence during the late winter. The year he went to Albany, he had to return to Waterville to convalesce for a few weeks in the early spring. It may have been tuberculosis, or an intractable cold weather catarrh, perhaps resulting in a chronic bronchitis or pneumonia. Before antibiotics, these conditions could be just as serious as tuberculosis. He was later to resign his positions in Albany and Portland to return to Waterville on the basis of health difficulties. Some writers have suggested he was consumptive, and there was indeed an epidemic of tuberculosis during those years, so that is not impossible. Yet Hall played the cornet for 31 years from 1874 until 1905, and it is not likely that tuberculosis would have permitted that. In the absence of medical records, we will probably never find out.

R B. Hall's fame began to spread as he appeared as a soloist at various locations away from the Richmond area. In 1876 (at the age of 18) he appeared in Old Orchard. [24] He was engaged as soloist for the summer season there in 1881. [25] He appeared as soloist at Nantasket beach, and became acquainted with Mace Gay who was the band leader at Nantasket Beach at that time. [26] Mace Gay, who in addition to leading the Martland band owned a publishing firm, later published many of Hall's marches.

During this time Hall is said to have been a part of Baldwin's Boston Cadet Band, to have met the world famous cornetist Allessandro Liberati and to have played alongside him. [27] According to Thomas C. Bardwell's widely quoted 1977 article for *Fanfare*, Hall's career in Boston extended from 1878 until 1882, and Hall spent these four seasons sharing the solo desk with Liberati in J. T. Baldwin's First Corps of Cadets Band. [28] However, because the years from 1878 to 1881 were the years when Sturtevant remembered Hall as leading the Richmond Cornet Band, Hall's Boston engagement could not have been during these earlier years. It must have come later, and been for one year, 1882. This agrees with

Bardwell's earlier article, in which he gives Hall one season, 1882, with the Baldwin Cadet Band. [29]

Because of the conflicting statements about this period in Hall's career, a review of Liberati's activities might provide some clues. According to band historian Glenn Bridges, Italian-born cornet virtuoso Allesandro Liberati (1847-1927) was cornet soloist with Baldwin's First Corps of Cadets Band in Boston in 1877 and 1878. During the following two seasons, however, he was soloist at Coney Island, New York. During the winter seasons of 1879 and 1880 Liberati was first cornet with the New York Philharmonic. In the ensuing seasons he played engagements in New York, Virginia and Chicago. [30]

Was the period that Hall played in Baldwin's Band four years (1878-1882 from age 20 to 24) as some contend, [31] or was it just one season, 1882, as others insist? [32] If Hall had been in Boston for four years, only the first of those would have been with Liberati; if Hall were with the Baldwin Cadet Band for only the season of 1882, then he may not have played assistant to Liberati at all, since Liberati was in Yorktown, Virginia, by then. If indeed Hall's apprenticeship in Boston had been four years, could he also have been founding, training, and leading the Richmond Cornet Band as well as appearing in Portland, Old Orchard, and Nantasket Beach during this

PLATE 5. R. B. HALL IN HIS EARLY TWENTIES (About 1880, Age 22). (Courtesy of Bagaduce Music Lending Library)

same period of time, as Sturtevant and Mansir reported? Four years seems a reasonable time for a musician to become a finished and polished artist; one year, considering his reputation as a natural virtuoso, might have been possible for Hall. Possibly he was performing in Boston some of the time, while training the band in Richmond in between Boston engagements.

It seems apparent that at the very least Hall played a whole season, 1882, with the Boston Cadet Band.[33] Hall's sporadic engagements in Nantasket Beach, Old Orchard Beach, Boston, and other places took place during the four years from 1878 to 1882, but he was based in Richmond, and returned to the Richmond Cornet Band regularly until late 1881. His year in Boston, 1882, followed. When Hall returned from the year in Boston, he was to leave Richmond behind, and base his career in Bangor, where he was engaged to play in Andrews' Orchestra beginning in December of 1882.

NOTES

1 Willam C. White, *A History of Military Music in America*, (New York: Exposition Press, 1945), 139-140.

2 Ralph Gould, "R. B. Hall - Maine's Music Man," *Down East*, October 1967, 30-33.

3 A letter substantiating the loss, dated June 10, 1964, written by Joseph Pecoraro, Superintendant of Schools, to Ralph Gould, is in the Hall collection, folder 2, at Bagaduce Music Lending Library, in Blue Hill, Maine.

4 Bardwell, *Fanfare*, 28.

5 White, op. cit., 139, and Bridges, *Pioneers in Brass*, 139.

6 Luther C. Bateman, "Maine's March King - Richmond Musician's Music Enjoyed by Royalty," *Lewiston* [Maine] *Journal*, 15 July 1922, M1-2. (Hereafter *LJ*).

7 Ibid.

8 Ibid.

9 George Thornton Edwards, *Music and Musicians of Maine*, (Portland, Maine: Southworth Press, 1928), 340.

10 Ralph Gould, "R. B. Hall - Maine's Music Man,"*Down East*, October 1967, 30-33.

11 Bateman, *LJ*, 15 July 1922.

12 Margaret Hindle Hazen and Robert M. Hazen, *The Music Men: An Illustrated History of Brass Bands in America, 1800-1920*, (Washington D. C.: Smithsonian Institution Press, 1987), xx, 7, 40.

13 Harry W. Schwartz, *Bands of America*, (Garden City, New York: Doubleday, 1957), 31.

14 Hazen, op. cit., 91-92.

15 Bateman, op. cit.

16 Louis Philippe Laurendau (1861-1916); composer, arranger, and music editor for Carl Fischer, Inc.

17 John Daly Fleming, ed. *Richmond on the Kennebec*, (Richmond, Maine: Richmond Historical Committee, 1966).

18 Bateman, op. cit.

19 Ibid.

20 Mildred Beedle Fossett, "Bowdoinham Man Was Most Noted March Composer", *Lewiston* [Maine] *Journal*, 22 March 1952, 3A.

21 Bateman, op. cit.

22 Fleming, *Richmond on the Kennebec*, 133.

23 Bateman, op. cit.

24 Bateman, op. cit.

25 White, op. cit., 139.

26 Gould, op. cit.

27 Robert Hudson, "R. B. Hall Day," *The Instrumentalist*, December 1983, 54-55.

28 Bardwell, *Fanfare*, (1977), 28.

29 Thomas C. Bardwell, Sr., "Robert Browne Hall: The New England March King," *Music Journal Anthology 1968*, ed. R. Cumming (New York, 1968), 33.

30 Glenn Bridges, *Pioneers in Brass*, (Detroit, Michigan: Sherwood Publications, 1965), 60-61.

31 Thomas C. Bardwell, Sr., "The New England March King," *Fanfare*, 1:10 (1977), 28.   Robert Hudson, "R. B. Hall Day," *The Instrumentalist*, December 1983, 54.   Robert F. Swift, "Credit Overdue: R. B. Hall," *Woodwind, Brass, Percussion*, November 1982, 20.

32 Luther C. Bateman, "Maine's March King: Richmond Musician's Music Enjoyed By Royalty" *Lewiston* [Maine] *Journal*, 15 July 1922, 1-2. Gould, op. cit.

33 Bateman, op. cit., and Gould, op. cit.

CHAPTER TWO
HALL'S ARRIVAL AND FIRST YEAR IN BANGOR
(1882-1883)

Because of the writings of some earlier authors, the contemporary impression has developed that R. B. Hall came to Bangor specifically to assume leadership of the Bangor Band, and that leading the band was his primary occupation for eight years. Bateman was practically quoting from the brief biography included in Hall's obituary when he wrote in 1922 that Hall was "called to Bangor as director of the leading band of that city. There he remained for eight years, and it was there that he began his work as a composer."[1]

When reworked thirty years later by Mildred Beedle Fossett this same thought was presented as follows: "The following year he returned to Maine as Director of the leading band in Bangor. He remained there eight years. It was there that he began composing marches in 1884."[2] In Gould's words this became: "The following year he was invited to conduct the Bangor Band. Hall remained in Bangor from 1883 until 1890, and there first seriously began composing."[3]

In 1982, University of New Hampshire Band Professor Robert F. Swift needed fresh prose for a journal article on Hall. Assembling what had already been written, but without the addition of any new information other than the inclusion of the title of Hall's first published march, *M.H.A.*, Swift's treatment added the weight of formality to Hall's relocation to Bangor.

...at which time he received an invitation to travel north to Bangor to lead the Municipal Band. This was in 1883. In 1884 he composed his first commercial march, and named it "M.H.A." [4]

Because of the recirculation of these same few sentences, a generation of band fans has had the impression that Hall's primary mission in Bangor was, as Bardwell put it, "to rebuild the Bangor Band."[5] While it is true that he did accomplish that task, we will see from contemporary newspaper accounts that his primary reason for coming to Bangor was that he was engaged by Melville H. Andrews to play in Andrews' Orchestra, the busiest dance orchestra in Bangor.

Andrews had led the Bangor Band for fifteen years until the summer before Hall's arrival, after which it had gone into a precipitous decline in prestige and activity under the leadership of W. B. Peakes. Once Hall was established in Bangor musical circles, Andrews introduced him to the men who were the nucleus of the band.

Hall began rehearsing the Bangor Band in January of 1883, a process which eventually resulted in an increase in size, importance, and activity for the band, and ultimately in Hall's reputation as having "rebuilt" it. The mainstay of his musical work during that time, however, was as cornet soloist in Andrews' Orchestra. His reputation as a cornetist had preceded him, and from his arrival in Bangor he impressed the public with his cornet solos.

HALL'S ARRIVAL IN BANGOR

Hall's career was already off to a flying start when he came to Bangor in the winter of 1882-3. Now 24 years old, he had just finished a lengthy engagement with Baldwin's Boston Cadet Band, and after a brief stop in Richmond, he came to spend the winter in Bangor.

At the time that he arrived in Bangor, Hall had already been introduced in the Bangor press. A piece a month earlier served to notify the public that Andrews had recently revamped his orchestra roster, and expanded from seven to twelve players. On October 27 the *Bangor Daily Commercial* reported that:

> *Mr. M. H. Andrews has reorganized his Orchestra with the following members: M. H. Andrews, first violin, leader and prompter; Charles Cushing, second violin; Fred F. Parks, viola; Dr. E. T. Wasgatt, cello; Eugene Haley, double bass; J. M. Mulally, Clarinet; R. B. Hall of the Boston Cadet Band, first cornet; J. B. Files, second cornet; Horace Woods, trombone, H. Andrews, Drum; J. G. Kimball, and George Cushing, pianists.[6]*

This prior announcement was sufficient to ensure that Hall's expected arrival in Bangor was noticed and reported when it occurred. The *Bangor Daily Commercial* for Saturday,

December 2, 1882, reported in "local matters" as follows:

> *Mr. R. B. Hall has arrived in the city and taken the place of B-flat cornetist in Andrews Orchestra. Mr. Hall has been in Baldwin's Boston Cadet Band of late. He is a fine cornetist and is well known in New England.[7]*

Several points of interest arise from these brief news announcements. Orchestra bookings must have been very good at the time for Andrews to nearly double the size (and therefore the expense of hiring) his orchestra. M. H. Andrews, Bangor's leading musician and most successful dancing teacher, had already hired Hall from Boston a full month before his arrival in Bangor. Hall was the only one of the musicians listed in the announcement to have a qualification mentioned: the others were all local figures, already well known to the Bangor public.

Over the next few weeks some mention of Hall's involvement in Andrews' Orchestra appeared in the *Commercial* about three times a week. Andrews' Orchestra was busy, and Hall's arrival had brought increased attention to its activities. Just five days after his arrival in the city, Hall played solos from the orchestra pit at a performance of the "New Magdalen," a stage play starring Miss Fanny Reeves, and given—with incidental music from the pit as was customary at the time—at the Bangor Opera House on December 7, 1882. The performance was announced in advance, for both Miss Reeves and Hall were attractions, and the *Commercial* reviewed the entire evening's entertainment as a success. According to the following day's paper:

The music by Andrews' Orchestra was unusually good, and the cornet solo by Mr. Hall was very fine. He was heartily encored, and responded.[8]

Only a few days later, a church concert at the Unitarian church featuring solos by Hall and Andrews to the accompaniment of Miss Garland on the church organ received a glowing review, and had an unusually large attendance in spite of the fact that the paper had reported unfavorable weather.[9]

This was the first of many collaborations of these two musicians. Abbie N. Garland (1852-1942) was to provide Hall's accompaniment many times during the ensuing decade, even after Hall's move to Waterville. In addition to being a church organist for more than 25 years, she was also director of the Bangor Piano School, and the composer of several once popular piano pieces. She was the pianist for Andrews' Orchestra when serious works were performed in conjunction with the Bangor Cecelia Club, often with Hall on the cornet. It is she who is credited with originating the organization of the Bangor Symphony Orchestra in 1896 and enlisting Horace M. Pullen as its first conductor.[10]

Andrews' Orchestra was called upon to provide the music for the Military and Civic Ball held in mid-December. Adjutant Henry L. Mitchell was to be general manager.[11] Col. Mitchell, a Civil War veteran who was a prominent Bangor attorney, later was promoted to General in the Maine Volunteer Militia. Also later he became a benefactor for the Bangor Band under Hall's leadership.

Hall was to write a march the following year, entitled *Col. Mitchell*. This piece was never published and shows evidence of Hall's earliest march style. Later some of the melodic ideas from this march were to surface in the *General Mitchell* march published in 1889 by Mace Gay.

Andrews' Orchestra and M. H. Andrews's extremely popular dancing classes were already receiving frequent brief newspaper mentions because of their active place in Bangor's entertainment scene at the time. Andrews' Orchestra played in the pit at the Bangor Opera House whenever the play or show required music. It also played for balls held by various groups throughout the city. The only real competition for these balls and casual engagements came from Rowe's Orchestra, which played the Brewer Social dances regularly. Howard's Orchestra was often reported as playing excursions and dances held outside of the city, but no major engagements in Bangor itself. The major entertainment on New Year's Eve, 1882, was a policeman's ball given at the Music Hall, with music by Andrews' Orchestra. Tickets were $1.00, a fairly steep price in those times, equivalent to a seat at the best theatrical productions.[12]

Hall's cornet solos from the Opera House pit began to attract attention as soon as he arrived in Bangor. By February 1883, it was an inducement to a larger attendance if the *Commercial* merely mentioned Hall's solos. The following preview is typical.

At the Opera House this evening the audience will be accorded between the acts, a musical treat from Andrews Full Orchestra, composed as follows: M. H. Andrews, director and 1st violin; Cushing, 2nd violin; Files, viola; Haley, double bass; Wasgatt, cello; Mulalley, clarinet; Hall, 1st. cornet; Files, 2nd. cornet; Woods, trombone; Adams, drum; Cushing, piano. Much of the music will be entirely new. Mr. Hall will probably render solos.[13]

Not only were Hall's solos a feature of the Opera House performances, but at dances he was featured, too. Wherever he played he was enthusiastically applauded and reviewed.

Introductory to the ball, last Monday evening Andrews' Orchestra gave a short concert. The selection was good, fairly rendered, and the large audience showed their appreciation by numerous encores and applause. The chief feature was the cornet playing of Mr. Hall, and especially the solos. This gentleman—a stranger for us—has a brilliant future before him in his profession. He is quite young, already ranks well, and we shall expect to see his name on the list of our prominent solo cornetists at no distant date. We hope to hear him again soon.[14]

Throughout the winter and spring, Hall's solos created a stir every time Andrews' Orchestra played (see photo, following). Hall was kept busy, since the orchestra played several engagements, whether dances or in the opera house, every week. As a rule the orchestra would play a short concert, about an hour, then there would be a dance, with the selections following a set order of waltzes, schottisches, polkas, a Boston fancy, a Portland fancy, etc. A grand march was often part of the festivities, especially at larger balls, lodge, and military balls.

The usual ensemble for dancing was a small orchestra of five to twelve players, but bands also played for dancing, especially at very large gatherings. Social dances such as the galop, galop-racket, polka, and one-step all had steps that were danced to marches of various characters.[15] A few years later, when the two-step became popular, six-eight marches became important as dance numbers; by the turn of the century quadrilles were in vogue, requiring marches with alternating strains of six-eight and two-four. As his career developed, Hall responded to these changing fashions, composing marches for the many dance styles of the organizations where he so frequently performed.

Although Hall's association with Bangor became known to later generations through his leadership of the Bangor Band, and the marches he composed for the Band and dedicated to Bangor luminaries, his original association with Bangor and the mainstay of his economic survival in his Bangor years, was, we have seen, as cornetist in Andrews' Orchestra.

Hall's marches and the Bangor Band have lived on to the present day. The Bangor Band was already incorporated long before Hall's arrival, and as a corporate entity it has weathered the winds of change, still giving concerts in the park as it did a hundred years ago. The majority of R. B. Hall's marches were copyrighted and published, and have been played world wide. They, too, have attained entity status, a life independent of their creator, and will be played as long as there are bands to play them.

In contrast, Andrews Orchestra, devoted to playing the popular melodies of the day for dancing, has faded from the scene, and is remembered only by devotees of old-time Bangor history. Andrews dismantled the orchestra in 1890 at the time he entered the music store business.[16] In its day, however, it was extremely popular, in constant demand, and the better money maker of the two groups. Such is still the relationship between dance orchestras and concert groups: although people enjoy both listening and dancing, as a rule they will readily pay more for music to dance to than they will for music to listen to. Concert organizations, however, have a more permanent repertoire, a more permanent place in the community, and a life that spans the generations.

Melville H. Andrews (1845-1921) could play the violin, cello, cornet, fife, and piano; taught dancing and ran dancing classes; directed the Bangor Band and played in and directed (1901-1904) the Bangor Symphony; ran a successful music store; and left a considerable fortune to Bangor musical groups when he passed away. He was Bangor's leading musical figure at the time.[17] He was a veteran of the Civil War, where he led the Twelfth Maine Regiment Band until 1866.[18] He founded Andrews Orchestra in Bangor in 1867, and was leader of the Bangor Band for fifteen years from 1867 until 1882, just a short time before R. B. Hall came to Bangor to join his orchestra (and soon took over the band.)

ndrews gave up the dance orchestra business at the time he acquired Wheelden's music store and from it established Andrews' Music House in 1890. Shortly thereafter he married Miss Helen Burton Nealley of Bangor. He composed two marches, *Pride of the Army* and *Pride of the Navy*, both of which were published by Carl Fischer in 1896, and two more marches (*American Legion*, 1918, and *Spirit of the Times*, 1921, published by Andrews Music House) as well as several other pieces late in his life. Although he once even conducted Sousa's Band in a performance of *Pride of the Army*, none of his marches are played any more. Even Andrews' Music House, a thriving music store and long a fixture of downtown Bangor, eventually went out of business. It disappeared from the scene in 1974.

THE BANGOR BAND AND HALL'S EARLY ROLE.

The Bangor Band was struggling at the time Hall arrived in Bangor, and had relatively few engagements. The bulk of the city's band engagements that winter were being filled by the Brewer Cornet Band, under the capable leadership of clarinetist J. M. Mulally. The City Directory for 1882 also lists the Saint John's Band, associated with Saint John's Commandery of Knights Templars; according to newspaper accounts they were also frequently engaged. The

Bangor Band, however, after a busy Fourth of July and a Handel Society excursion aboard the steamer "Katahdin,"[19] was reported only 26as "practicing industriously."[20]

The Bangor Band's decline came about rather suddenly in the summer of 1882, when Andrews, who had led the band for the previous fifteen years, took a summer position at the Oceanic and Appledore Hotels on the Isles of Shoals, off the New Hampshire coast. The band was left to the leadership of W. B. Peakes, who had played in the band since Civil War days. Although they may have had some other engagements during the summer of 1882, none were of sufficient prominence to be mentioned in the newspaper. In sharp contrast, the following year with Hall in charge of the band, there were at least two engagements a week of sufficient importance to be included in the local news. By 1884, with concerts in the park, at the Bangor House[21], at Norombega Hall,[22] and excursions and picnics, the Bangor Band had an almost daily presence in the news.

In Andrews' Orchestra, R. B. Hall met the men who formed the nucleus of the Bangor Band: Woods, Files, Cushing, Wasgatt, and Mulally. Years later he was to hire these same men, with the inclusion of Eugene A. Haley, a double-bass player who played an E-flat Helicon bass in the band, to come to Waterville to augment his Waterville Military

PLATE 6. R. B. HALL IN HIS TWEN-TIES (About 1883, Age 25) (Courtesy of Bagaduce Music Lending Library)

Band for special occasions such as Colby College commencement concerts. Hall soon assumed band leadership, and began the process of instructing and revitalizing. An item in the *Bangor Daily Commercial* dated January 8, 1883, roughly a month after Hall's arrival in the city, states: "The Bangor Band will hold a full rehearsal Tuesday evening.

The instruction by Mr. R. B. Hall is productive of the best effort."[23]

Hall's style as a band leader was that of a teacher or trainer. He taught the men how to play, and was evidently not only very patient and demanding, as Sturtevant's memoirs from Richmond have pointed out, but also personable and gracious. Years later Dr. Fred E. Maxfield, who played cornet in the Bangor Band beginning in 1884 and continuing throughout the Hall era, was to give the following reminiscence to a reporter:

He had a delightful personality—was easy to know and talk with. He could impart his knowledge very gracefully—had a good sense of humor, too. As a leader he was no driver, but always had things under control. Musicians not only respected him—they loved him—and he inspired them to do their best.[24]

While in Bangor, Hall was famed as an improviser, not in jazz, as bandsmen today often improvise, but in the waltzes, schottisches and variation forms of his era. Again according to Maxwell, as told to Fuller:

He was given to 19th century style jam sessions when playing with J. J. Mulalley, top Bangor area Clarinetists [sic].[25] On dance dates each would try to outdo the other with improvisations.[26]

HALL AND THE BANGOR BAND IN THE FIRST YEAR

Throughout the months of January, February, and March, 1883, the Bangor Band did not perform, confining its efforts to rehearsing under Hall's tutelage once or twice a month. Hall, meanwhile, was very busy with Andrews' Orchestra, playing almost nightly, and soloing several times a week. In spite of the fact that the winter of 1883 was an unusually cold one, the Brewer Band and the Winterport Cornet Band all had occasional publicized engagements. The Bangor Band came alive only in late March, when rehearsals began to be held weekly, then twice-weekly as April began.

After a rehearsal on Saturday, March 31, and again on Tuesday, April 3, the band gave a short serenade on the steps of the Bangor House. The following day an announcement of the band's reorganization appeared in the *Commercial*. The band must have liked the results of Hall's instruction, for they hired him for the season. This was front page news.

The Bangor Band has engaged Mr. R. B. Hall, the well-known cornet soloist, for the coming year beginning on May 1st. Mr. Hall says that he intends to have as fine a band organization as there is in Maine. The Band will give concerts each week during the summer in the park. The Band

last evening reorganized and elected the following officers: Mr. R. B. Hall, musical conductor and agent; W. Milton, president; Wm. A. Palmer, clerk; P. F. Todd, treasurer; Standing committee, T. Gallagher, H. A. Adams, F. Clark. After the rehearsal last evening the band played several selections outdoors.[27]

Noteworthy in this announcement is the fact that Hall was made agent from the beginning, and named conductor, not merely instructor, as was later to be the case during his first year in Waterville. The level of activity during that first summer indicates that he took that role very much to heart. Also of interest is the fact that the officers were not the orchestra-men and full-time musicians, but rather the businessmen in the group. Of all the men mentioned in this announcement Hall is the only one familiar from lists of musicians and other musical programs of the day.

Two weeks later the first major appearance of the band under its new management produced a mixed result. A concert and dance were scheduled for Thursday, April 19, in Norumbega Hall. The *Commercial* forecast a large turnout: "As this is to be the first public appearance of the band there will be much interest in the concert and attendance will be large."[28] The following day ticket prices were announced, 25 cents for the concert and

50 cents additional for the dance, with Andrews' Orchestra, afterwards. The date, Maundy Thursday, the day of the "last supper," turned out to be unpropitious for such an affair, for Governor Robie declared a day of "fasting, humiliation, and prayer." Four other musical events, including the Virginia Jubilee Singers, were also presented in Bangor on the same evening.[29] A front page review the following day praised the performance but lamented the small turnout.

The Bangor Band under its present organization made its first appearance in public last evening in a concert in Norombega.[30] The excellent concert was deserving of an audience limited only by the capacity of the hall, and it is a matter of regret that so few were present. The playing of the band was highly creditable and surprised all that have not been aware that the members have been faithfully practicing under the instruction of Mr. R. B. Hall. The volume of sound and the melody were especially noticeable. It is an organization that before long will be second to no band in the state, and ought to have the generous support of our citizens. The numbers on the program were well executed. We understand that the band will give another concert before long, and if so there should be a large audience present. Mr. Hall played a solo "Palm Branches" and in response gave an encore "Yankee

March, "Hot Shot"	Rollinson
Overture, "Le Diadem"	Herman
Cornet Solo, "Palm Branches"	R. B. Hall, arranged by Mr. Hall
Schottische, "Sweet Sixteen"	Rollinson
Potpourri, "American Airs"	
Cornet Solo, "Two Friends"	Messrs. Hall and Tuck
Paraphrase, "Jerusalem the Golden"	Rollinson
Galop	Rollinson

PROGRAM FOR THE BANGOR BAND CONCERT, THURSDAY, APRIL 19, 1883. From the Bangor Daily Commercial review, 20 April 1883, page 1.

Doodle" with variations. The applause through the evening was frequent and hearty.[31]

The enthusiasm of the reviewer's tone is unmistakable in this piece. The goal of having the best band in the state was important to the public, and the reviewer assures that this will soon be so, while seeking support for the band. The mention of Hall's encore is important, because it is not mentioned on the program, yet this is one of Hall's solos for which the music is still extant. The program was presented in the newspaper in its entirety.[32]

Noteworthy on this program is the reliance on Connecticut bandmaster and prolific composer T. H. Rollinson (1844-1928) for tuneful and not too difficult material for the developing band. Also of interest are the cornet solos, chosen from among the same ones Hall had been performing all spring with Andrews. "Two Friends," performed with Frank Tuck who played second cornet with Andrews, was a feature to be repeated at both band and orchestra concerts for the next several years. The piano accompaniment part in Hall's hand is still extant (at Bagaduce) but no trace of the solo parts is to be found. The "Yankee Doodle Variations" given as an encore was especially arranged for Hall by J. Sproul. It is fast, florid and brilliant, requiring a technically solid player. It covers a range from G below the treble staff to D above. The manuscript cornet part is marked: "For R. B. Hall, Esq., but not transferrable." It was one of Hall's favorite encores, ranking with and similar to the "Carnival of Venice." It can be seen as part of the Hall collection at the Bagaduce Music Lending Library in Blue Hill, Maine.

From that concert on throughout the summer, the Bangor Band was increasingly more active. Hall's presence and instruction were warmly appreciated by the band and the community, and M. H. Andrews began a plan to offer a testimonial and public appreciation of Hall's presence that was intended to induce him to wish to remain in Bangor more permanently. The following week the first inklings of the Hall testimonial were printed. "The date of the benefit," said the *Commercial*, would "soon be announced."[33] As the season unfolded, this was to be postponed many times. A month later it was announced that the benefit would be "postponed until fall." A new touch was included: "At that time," the *Commercial* continued, "a first class cornet will be given."[34] It would not be until July of 1884 that this event was actually to come to pass.

During the remainder of the season the band circulated a petition to raise money to help pay Hall's salary. The goal was to become one of the best bands in the state and the band was very active in that pursuit. The Bangor Band adopted the name "Bangor Military Band," a reflection on the idea that their instrumentation should include a substantial number of woodwinds to balance the sound, as opposed to a "cornet band" (as the Bangor Band had been until 1877) which would have been at least nominally all brass and percussion. They did not change the incorporated name of the band, however, nor did they repaint the bass drum head. In photographs from the era it still proclaims simply "Bangor Band."

The idea of a "military" rather than "cornet" band was to become a key element in Hall's style as a leader and as a composer. A few years later, within a short time of Hall's taking over its tutelage, the Waterville City Band became the Waterville Military Band.

Pictures of Hall's bands show the Bangor "Military" Band, the Waterville Military Band and the Richmond (Cornet) Band as predominantly brass, with a few clarinets and a piccolo. Although Hall's bands usually numbered between twenty and thirty players and typically had only four or five woodwind players at most, his musical concept included parts for a reed section appropriate for a much larger band. Even though he seldom had flutes and never had saxophones in his band, these timbres fit well into his concept and publishers were later able to add the parts as these instruments came into use. Hall's emphasis on the trend to including more reeds is another reason why his marches have been so enduring. As bands have gotten bigger, the proportion of woodwinds has increased, coming closer to the ideal instrumentations chosen by Sousa and Gilmore.

As the summer of 1883 progressed, the Bangor Band gave concerts in the park weekly or more frequently. Programs were not printed, but the *Commercial* always noticed and mentioned the band's appearances, even if space did not always permit a full review.

The summer season in the region was not spent in musical isolation, for visiting talent of all kinds came to Bangor. Bands were among the kinds of entertainment included; Hall and the Bangor Band had the opportunity to hear and be heard by two fine groups that season. When the Boston Cadet Band came to Bangor, accompanying the Worcester, Massachusetts, Commandery of Knights Templar on their summer pilgrimage by steamer, both bands played in the street parade.[35] On the Fourth of July, the Bangor Band paraded with 24 pieces, while the 62nd Fusiliers Band, visiting the city, paraded with 21 pieces.[36]

Once M. H. Andrews left the city for his summer job on the Isles of Shoals, Hall's work with the orchestra was infrequent, but the band took up the slack, playing excursions down the Penobscot River to Fort Point, Islesboro, Northport, Lincolnville, and other favorite destinations. Sometimes these excursions were undertaken by a club or organization. At other times they were public, and took on as many as 500 paying guests. The band played on at least one, and more often two or three of these outings every week during the season. As is the case with today's "tourist season" in Maine, the "excursion season" of a century ago began immediately after July 4, reached its peak in mid-August, and concluded fairly abruptly in mid-September.

On one such excursion Hall and the Bangor Band accompanied a full load of passengers on the steamer "Penobscot" for an extended day-trip to Squirrel and Mouse Islands and Boothbay Harbor. The "Penobscot" left the dock at 4 o'clock Sunday morning with guests aboard who had already started the party on Saturday night. Staterooms were reserved in advance. The band played on the boat ride, and in Boothbay as well. On the return trip the Bangor Band "furnished excellent music under the leadership of R. B. Hall" while an "excellent supper" was served to the "large crowd."[37] The steamer arrived back at the dock in Bangor on Monday morning about 2:00 a.m.

Meanwhile, for much of July attention was turned to the forthcoming annual band tournament to be held at the resort at Lake Maranacook. Located near Winthrop, Maine, (just west of Augusta) this popular resort destination was right on the railroad line, and attracted thousands from all over the state to a wide variety of programs including concerts, lectures, sailing regattas (with band accompaniment) and religious and spiritual programs. One of the most popular of these events was the great band tournament. Chandler's and Glover's bands were to square off at the band contest at Maranacook, since they were popularly held to be the two best bands in the state. News accounts described the forthcoming duel in almost pugilistic metaphors.

With only three days remaining before the contest, Glover's Band pulled out leaving the top spots in the challenge to Chandler's and the Bangor Band. The public was led to expect a head-to-head duel. Enthusiasm for the contest ran high, and the journalism got nastier.

Glover's acknowledges that it has beaten small country bands to call itself the champion, but will not take on the better bands, Bangor, and Chandler's.

Some of the organizations that want to "down" Chandler's should challenge the Bangor Band—if they want to get left.[38]

As it turned out, Chandler's Band, too, pulled out of the competition, and the Bangor Band wisely opted to take a well-paid engagement for an excursion on the steamer "Ralph Ross" and barge "Clifford" to Islesboro and Northport. After all the hype and inflated expectations, a crowd of 10,000 turned out at the tournament to hear a small band from Westbrook win the $100 first prize over five other small country bands. Chandler's Band "as the past winner" gave a demonstration concert after the contest was over.[39] It was not until years later that the competitors would finally meet at Maranacook. Glover's Band was soon to come to Bangor, however, as part of the Odd Fellows parade later that same season.

In other news that summer Col. H. L. Mitchell appointed Olin B. Bridge, a Bangor man, to the post of Adjutant to the Second Regiment.[40] This move paved the way for the Bangor Band to receive a regimental appointment when it became available the following spring. Hall's march *Adjutant Bridge* was premiered the following season. His *Second Regiment* (unpublished) appears to have been written at about the same time.

The Winterport band announced its intention to hire Hall as instructor for the following fall and winter. Hall accepted, and as the fall progressed also announced that he would teach the Dexter Band during the winter. The Odd Fellows parade in September featured Glover's Band with 22 men, and the Bangor Band, 24 men.

Throughout the fall, no further word of the testimonial for Hall was heard, and—once Andrews returned to the city— orchestra business began to increase, supplanting band business as winter approached. The Bangor Band stayed busy nevertheless, playing for ice skating at the new skating rink at Norumbega. This kept the band together and playing through the winter, ensuring a quick start to the concert season the following spring. One little announcement in the paper at the end of October was designed to catch the attention of anyone interested in a gold cornet.

A fine gold plated cornet on exhibition in the window of Pol's jewelry store attracts much attention. It was made by Isaac Fiske of Worcester Mass, and is an elegant instrument. For further particulars inquire of Mr. M. H. Andrews.[41]

Later news would show that Andrews had been taking up a collection to acquire a fine cornet for Hall's testimonial, but whether this was the same cornet cannot be said for certain. We know that Hall's cornet was manufactured by the Boston Musical Instrument Company. Perhaps Isaac Fiske was the engraver or the gold-plater. It is also possible that this was not destined to be Hall's cornet. If so, perhaps Andrews did not find it suitable; or he may have sold it to someone else. Hall would be awarded his cornet the following summer, but as 1883 drew to a close, and the outdoor band season was over, his attention turned to more orchestra work and theater pit playing.

Hall's career as it developed through the years had a cyclical nature. This was due to the annual cycle of the music business at the time. Band work predominated in the summer months when outdoor concerts and excursions provided lucrative opportunities for employment. During the winter, dance orchestra and theater work was more plentiful. Teaching music lessons and training bands, a winter occupation, was also important to Hall, but these activities were less lucrative than band and orchestra work. Later in his career Hall was likely to seek a change of location during the winter months. During the winter of 1883-1884 in Bangor, Hall turned his attention to composing his first commercially successful marches.

NOTES

[1] Luther C. Bateman, "Maine's March King," *Lewiston Journal*, (15 July 1922).

[2] Mildred Beedle Fossett, "Bowdoinham Man Was Among Most Noted March Composers," *Lewiston Journal*, Magazine Section, 22 March 1952.

[3] Ralph T. Gould, "R. B. Hall, Maine's Music Man," *Down East Magazine*, October 1967, 30.

[4] Robert F. Swift, "Credit Overdue: R. B. Hall," *Woodwind, Brass, and Percussion*, 21, no. 7 (November 1982): 20.

[5] Thomas C. Bardwell, Sr., "The New England March King," *Fanfare*, 1:10 (1977), 28-30.

[6] Bangor [Maine] Daily Commercial, 27 October 1882, 2. (Hereafter BDC)

[7] *BDC*, 2 December 1882, 3.

[8] *BDC*, 8 December 1882, 2.

[9] *BDC*, 11 December 1882, 2.

[10] Edwards, op. cit., 114, 178, 179, 277, 281, 397.

[11] *BDC*, 19 December 1882, 2.

[12] *BDC*, 7 December 1882, 3.

[13] *BDC*, 8 February 1883, 1.

[14] *BDC*, 10 February 1883, 4.

[15] Complete instructions for these and other dance steps of the era can be found in: J. Tillman Hall, *A Complete Guide to Social, Folk, And Square Dancing* (Belmont, CA: Wadsworth Publishing Co., 1963), 195,196.

[16] *BDC*, 24 February 1921.

[17] *BDC*, 24 February 1921.

[18] Edwards, op. cit., 283-4.

[19] *BDC*, 22 July 1882.

[20] *BDC*, 2 September 1882.

[21] The Bangor House was a Hotel located at the corner of Main and Union Streets in Bangor. It was Bangor's most prominent and luxurious hotel at the time.

[22] Norombega Hall was situated between Franklin and Central Streets, on a granite foundation in the Kenduskeag Stream. Its street level was a market place; its upper level had galleries and a stage, and could seat more than twenty-five hundred people, for concerts, plays and presentations of all types. Abigail Ewing Zelz and Marilyn Zoidis, *Woodsmen and Whigs: Historic Images of Bangor*, (Virginia Beach, VA: The Donning Co., 1991), 35.

[23] *BDC*, 8 January 1883, 4.

[24] John Fuller, "Hall Composed Music To Beat The Band," *Portland* [Maine] *Sunday Telegram*, 26 October 1958, 1D.

[25] Actually the name should be J. M. Mulalley.

[26] Ibid.

[27] *BDC*, 4 April 1883, 1.

[28] *BDC*, 16 April 1883, 1.

[29] *BDC*, 17 April 1883, 1,4.

[30] The standard spelling is now Norumbega, but a century ago it was not so standard. Norembega, Norombega, and Noronbega were frequently seen in news stories and advertisements. When it first appeared on Verrazzano's 1524 map it was spelled "Aranbega." The building in Bangor was named Norombega Hall. Hall's 1895 march was *Norembega*.

[31] *BDC*, 20 April 1883, 1.

[32] Ibid.

[33] *BDC*, 25 April 1883, 4.

[34] *BDC*, 26 May 1883, 1.

[35] *BDC*, 21 June 1883, 1.

[36] *BDC*, 5 July 1883, 1.

[37] *BDC*, 23, 24, 25 August 1883.

[38] *BDC*, 14 July 1883.

[39] *BDC*, 18 July 1883.

[40] *BDC*, 18 August 1883, 1.

[41] *BDC*, 30 October 1883, 4.

CHAPTER THREE

THE HALL TESTIMONIAL AND HALL'S YEARS IN BANGOR (1884-1889)

In 1884 the citizens of Bangor presented R.B. Hall with a Boston Three Star "Ne Plus" cornet, gold plated and lavishly engraved. It was perhaps the finest available in its day, and was the type preferred by the greatest cornet virtuosi. Alessandro Liberati and Herbert L. Clarke are two of the world-famous players who preferred the Boston Three Star. Hall played this cornet for the rest of his life, and even though he was given others, it remained his preferred instrument.[1] This is the cornet which is on display at the Waterville Historical society, along with Hall's shaving mug. Hall is said to have written his march *Greeting To Bangor* in response to this occasion, although it was not published for a decade.[2]

The events leading up to the testimonial week capped a very busy spring for Hall and the Bangor Band. With the training and rehearsal season for the Winterport and Dexter Bands nearing their end, Hall's work centered around the Bangor Band which was preparing for the summer season in April; and on Andrews' Orchestra, now busier than ever.

As the band season grew nearer Hall fed an occasional bit of band news to the Commercial, in order to get the public thinking about band concerts again. A short announcement in the "local brevities" department on April 17 heralded a change in Hall's career.

Mr. R. B. Hall the cornet player has written several marches which will be played by the Bangor Band the coming summer. They are said to be fine productions.[3]

Heretofore Hall had been known only as a cornet player, soloist, and band leader. He had written some arrangements for the bands he led, and also three marches titled simply with the initials of the Richmond Cornet Band, *R.C.B.1, R.C.B.2,* and *R.C.B.3.* These had been hand-copied into the band books of the Richmond players, but were not really finished products. The early "R.C.B." marches were later reworked and published under other titles.

H all had been trying his hand at various styles of composing, as some of the scraps of his youthful attempts that have surfaced in later years indicate, but none of these had more than a hint of what was to become his mature style.[4] Now, with these new pieces crafted in the winter of 1884, Hall would begin to be known as a composer of marches.

During the next 21 years Hall was to create the marches that became familiar to bandsmen all over America and around the world. Ultimately he would earn the sobriquet "Maine's March King" from the Waterville press, and posterity would remember him mainly for his marches. During his second year in Bangor, however, he was probably more concerned with improving the Bangor Band and playing the busy summer season.

The first of the new marches to be performed was *Adjutant Bridge* on May 27, 1884. This was the Bangor Band's first open air concert of the season, and the program was published in advance in the Commercial, a novelty for the Bangor Band for that time.[5]

This program is interesting because of the many relatively easy pieces which indicates a level of achievement that, while it was said to be a considerable advance for the band, nevertheless was nothing like the programs that

1. March	"Gen. Wales"	Missud
2. Selection	"Maritania"	Arr. J.B. Claus
3. Waltz	"Bride of the Night"	Lamotte
4. March	"Adj. Bridge" (first time)	R. B. Hall
5. Medley	"Recollections of the War"	Beyer
6. Serenade	"My Dream"	Missud
7. Galop	"Bacchanal"	Rollinson

Program of the May 27, 1884 Bangor Band concert, as published in the Bangor Daily Commercial, 27 May 1884

Hall was able to produce with the Bangor Band or the Waterville Military Band in later years. It is especially memorable, however, because it is the first program on which a Hall march is named, and declared to be a premier.

The review on the following day praised the band's accomplishment, and opined that "it was a surprise to many to find that the band could play so well."[6] The editors went on to describe the band's rapid improvement under Hall's tutelage. Plans were announced for an open air concert every week in Centre Park. A separate article on page four decried the disruption caused by rowdies during the concert, and chided the city for failure to provide adequate police protection during the concert. The editors hoped that the situation would be remedied by the following week.[7]

The busy spring for the band was made even busier by the Penobscot River excursion season being shifted ahead. More business than usual was being done in June and July because of the State's experiment with a closed season on lobsters from August 15 through November 15.[8] Usually, August was the peak of the excursion season, and many excursions included a clam and lobster bake at Lincolnville, Islesboro, Fort Point, or Northport. This year, however, was to be different because of the conservation experiment. With excursions coming at the start of the concert season, the band was busy indeed.

One of the very few insights into Hall's personal life was given on July 2, when the paper carried front page news of Hall, the sportsman. One sentence was all: "Mr. R. B. Hall, the cornet player, shot a loon at Pushaw yesterday."[9] Pushaw Pond, a large shallow lake about five miles west of Bangor, was a popular place to go hunting or fishing, and then as now, site of many summer homes, commonly called "camps" in Maine. That night (July 1) there was a band concert, and the following day it was back to music, as the Cecelia Club approached Hall to be its conductor in the following year.

The famed gold cornet was actually presented at a Thursday evening testimonial, July 10, 1884. This came at the end of a very busy Fourth of July week in which Hall and the band had played engagements on the third, Fourth, eighth and eleventh. Andrews' Orchestra had featured Hall as a soloist at a fancy dress ball in Ellsworth on the Fourth, in addition to his Bangor Band appearance earlier in the day. Although Andrews was due to leave for his summer job the following day (on July fifth) the *Bangor Daily Commercial* placed him in Ellsworth that night with Cushing, Files and Woods. Dr. Wasgatt was not present, having been hit in the eye with a piece of scraped tartar while working on a patient about two weeks previously, and still recuperating from the serious infection that nearly resulted in the loss of his eye. R. B. Hall played "Lizzie Polka," and was encored so insistently that he played "The Palm Branches" and "Then You'll Remember Me" before the audience would let him rest.[10] This was probably the last solo engagement that he played on his old cornet.

The band engagement two days later was an excursion with the Unitarian Society and Sunday School by steamer and barge to Fort Point for a picnic and dance. This was an all-day and evening affair, from which the boats (the steamer "Ralph Ross" and the barge "Clifford") returned late at night.

The testimonial itself was sandwiched between other band and musical activities for Hall, and held on Thursday evening, probably because of the excursion Wednesday and the Bangor Band concert scheduled for Friday evening. It was reported at length in the following day's *Commercial*.[11]

M. H. Andrews, who was again spending the summer as music director at the Oceanic Hotel, Isles of Shoals, sent a letter to accompany the gift. The letter was undated.

The letter was published in its entirety in the Bangor Daily Commercial for July 11, 1884, along with a brief congratulatory article. The published version differed in one or two words and some punctuation from the

---

Mr. R. B. Hall
Bangor, Maine

Dear Sir:

It is with feelings of pleasure that I present you the accompanying testimonial of the interest in and the kindly feeling entertained toward you by the citizens of Bangor. Since coming among us, you have made many warm friends, and won the admiration of all by your almost faultless execution upon the cornet, and wishing in some degree to express our gratitude for the pleasure you have afforded us we ask you to accept this cornet in token of our regard for you as a gentleman and musician.And whenever you awaken its golden tones remember that in every honorable undertaking you will have the cordial and hearty support of all. I but voice the sentiment of the community in expressing the hope that you will remain with us for many years.

Most sincerely
M. H. Andrews

TEXT OF THE LETTER accompanying the gift of the famed gold cornet to R. B. Hall from his supporters. As quoted in the Bangor Daily Commercial, 11 July, 1884.

original, which was written on Oceanic Hotel stationery and preserved in Fred Maxwell's collection, but the two versions are essentially identical.[12] Under Andrews' name in the newspaper version was the ascription: "For Subscribers to Testimonial," an acknowledgement that the presentation was not entirely Andrews' doing.[13] The testimonial article itself included the following words of praise for Hall and the cornet:

The friends and admirers of Mr. R. B. Hall, the talented cornet player, have presented him with an elegantly engraved gold cornet. It was manufactured by the Boston Musical Instrument Company. The tone of the cornet is pure and sweet, and it is as fine an instrument as there is in the country. In workmanship it is a credit to the Boston Musical Instrument Company, which deservedly has such a fine reputation. Mr. Hall is to be congratulated upon receiving such a handsome recognition of his talent and popularity.[14]

Hall wrote a letter of appreciation that was also printed in the newspaper that evening, and is the only example of Hall's letter writing to survive the century:

Bangor July 11, 1884

Mr. M. H. Andrews

MY DEAR SIR: -it is with deep feelings of thankfulness that I express to you and many friends the gratitude which I feel for the present of the elegant gold cornet and the accompanying testimonial. I feel highly complimented to be assured that I have met with the approval of the citizens of Bangor. Hereafter I shall labor with renewed zeal in order to retain their good will, and wherever I may be, I shall always remember them with the most kindly feelings. In this way I desire to express to you, personally, my heartfelt thanks for the interest taken in my behalf.

Very Sincerely Yours

R. B. HALL[15]

Coming as it did after a year-long build up, the gift of the gold cornet was certainly no surprise to Hall, yet it was a gesture which obviously touched him. His letter shows genuine appreciation despite a slight awkwardness with words that points to a personality much more practiced in musical expression than verbal skills. There was no time out for reflection, though, because the Bangor Band, with Hall leading and playing his cornet as usual, gave a concert at the Bangor House that

PLATE 7: R. B. HALL with Boston Three Star Cornet (from the collection of the author)

very night, "which was largely attended."[16] As they were in the middle of the busy summer season, Hall and the band then turned to the excursion business again as they accompanied The United Friends on an overnight excursion aboard the steamer "Katahdin" for which all the staterooms had been booked in advance for nearly six weeks. No sooner had they returned than they departed again with another church group, the Central Street Church, to Fort Point and Lincolnville Beach, once again on the steamer "Katahdin," for a picnic and dance.

At the very end of July, 1884, another event occurred that would eventually generate a Hall march title. The new Kineo House at Moosehead Lake was opened with great publicity following a year-long effort to rebuild it after the old Kineo Hotel had been destroyed by fire. A special Bangor and Piscataquis Railroad train was engaged for an overnight excursion to the grand opening, and the list of passengers seemed to be a Who's Who of Maine politicians and lawyers. Included in the list of dignitaries were Ex-Chief Justice (of the Maine Supreme Court) John Appleton, and journalist H. C. Wing of the Commercial. Three musicians were also named: R. B. Hall, Eugene Haley, and Horace Woods, all of the Bangor Band.[17] When they arrived at Kineo, they joined J. M. Mulally, who had arrived earlier, and orchestra leader H. M. Pullen, from Augusta, with his pianist, G. M. Prim. "The critical audience was much pleased with the rendering of the music," acknowledged the Commercial in a front page follow-up story after the revelers returned to Bangor.[18]

Several elements in this event had consequences in Hall's future activities. After the grand opening party, Pullen, the violinist and orchestra leader from Augusta, remained at Kineo, where he was engaged to direct the music for the entire summer. Hall was to return many times over the years to play with Pullen at the Kineo house. Additionally, Hall was later to play for Pullen's Orchestra at special events during his years in Waterville. Later (in 1896) Pullen was the first conductor of the Bangor Symphony Orchestra.

Having grown up on the banks of the Kennebec River, Hall had a special affinity for small boats, and was later to build several sailing canoes that he used during his stays at Kineo.[19] Journalist H. C. Wing who accompanied the excursion was later to become publisher of the Waterville Mail during Hall's years there. That might explain the similarity of the editorials pleading for support of the Bangor Band, to those later ones encouraging donations to the Waterville Military Band.

Hall's march Kineo was published by Mace Gay of Brockton, Massachusetts, in 1889. It was a very small arrangement that has to be augmented to be played by a present day full band.[20] The second strain includes a signal-like figure for the cornets that is echoed by the trombones, and is reminiscent of calling greetings out over the water, or perhaps of an echo from the lake.

BANGOR BAND LEADERSHIP AND THE SECOND REGIMENT APPOINTMENT.

Although later biographics summarize Hall's leadership of the Bangor Band as a solid block of eight years beginning in 1883, a closer inspection reveals that his involvement was more sporadic. It coincided with the band's activities as a regimental band, and the support generated by prominent citizens such as Bangor attorney (Second Regiment Colonel and, finally, General) Henry L. Mitchell. The Band's official history (written by A. W. Sprague in 1949) mentions Hall as leader for only a short stint, and the extensive summary of bands and commercial orchestras at the time by George Thornton Edwards gives Hall only two or three years with the Bangor Band. Although he does not specifically rule out other years of leadership for Hall, only 1883-4 and 1886 are enumerated. According to Edwards:

In 1883 R. B. Hall was elected leader. In 1884 the Band received the Second Regiment appointment and during the campaign which followed it was presented by the Loyal League with a bass drum, which it still has in its possession. In 1885 John Mullaly was leader, but in the following year R. B. Hall was again chosen, and he was succeeded by Frank L. Tuck.[22]

The bass drum mentioned above is prominently displayed in a photograph, taken in August, 1884, while the band was at the Second Regiment muster in Augusta, Maine. This very excellent photograph of the Bangor Band shows Hall as leader of the twenty-three piece band standing in the back row in the same uniform as the other men and holding a cornet, not a baton. All the men are shown with their instruments and are identified with a numbered key and list of names. This photo was reproduced for the cover of the reissued collection "R. B. Hall and the State Of Maine" produced in 1985 from photocopies of Hall's out-of-print Maine marches by

EXAMPLE 1. Kineo March by R. B. Hall, measures 21-38 of the solo cornet part. The calling motif is represented in the cue notes.[21]

Bangor Band tuba player and Bangor physician Dr. James D. Clement, Jr.

Just prior to leaving for summer military duty at Camp Robie in Augusta, Hall had been named "principal musician and band master of the Second Regiment" by Col. Mitchell.[23] Although the company was originally to be in camp for three weeks, they ultimately stayed only five days. The Bangor Band led the regiment in a parade from the train station in Augusta to Camp Robie on August 4, 1884. Total muster of the troops was 322, of which the band accounted for 24 (someone must have been absent from the picture). Both the Bangor Band and the Jameson Guards—Bangor's Company G— were reported as arriving back in Bangor on Saturday, August 9.[24]

The need for band music was such that when the Bangor Band was out of town, even for a few days, a vaccuum was created that had to be filled. During the week that the Bangor Band was in Augusta the newly-formed Citizen's Band, under J. M. Mullaly, received extra publicity as they filled engagements in Bangor. As soon as Hall and his band were back from camp they embarked on a steamer trip to Pemaquid, where Hall premiered a new march, this one titled *Unique.*[25] *Unique* has not survived to the present, and no manuscript or printed music for it can be found.

Edwards' summary of Bangor Band history notwithstanding, memorabilia in the band's collection indicate a longer and more extensive, if still sporadic, record of leadership for Hall. According to bandroom records, Hall's dates as conductor of the Bangor Band are 1882-3 through 1884; 1886; and 1893.[26]

Photographs of Bangor Band leaders, with their dates of office written on labels indicate an alternation between Hall and various others. Clarinetist John M. Mulally led the band during 1885. During the early 1880's Mulally was leader of the Brewer Band. Mulally had come to Bangor in about 1877 from Portland where he had been a member of Chandler's Band, and of the social dance orchestra known as "Chandler's Crack Six." Like Hall, he played in Andrews' Orchestra.

Hall was reelected leader in 1886. A succession of other leaders then took charge of the band during the remainder of the 1880's. Hall was succeeded as director of the Bangor Band in 1887 by the English cornet virtuoso Steven Crean, to whom Hall had dedicated a march for Bangor's Memorial Day parade.[27] Although highly respected in Bangor, Crean (who is sometimes also known as Cream) left after one year to return to England.

BANGOR BAND, MUSTER OF 2d REGIMENT, AUGUSTA, AUGUST, 1884

| 1 | 2 | 3 | 4 | 5 | 6 | 7 | 8 | 9 | 10 | 11 | 12 | | 13 |

14   15   16   17   18

19   20   21   22   23

1.E.A.Haley	7.J.Delaney	12.O.C.Drinkwine	18.F.E.Maxfield
2.Violet	8.R.B.Hall	13.J.G.Fenno	19.J.Philbrook
3.G.Cushing	(Leader)	14.J.McNulty	20.Job Springer
4.H.F.Woods	9.F.L.Tuck	15.P.H.Fenno	21.J.F.Todd
5.C.D.Bradman	10.H.D.Adams	16.Wm.Haly	22.G.M.Tuck
6.J.O.Files	11.T.J.Gallagher	17.Wm.Herrin	23.F.M.Clark

PLATE 8 THE BANGOR BAND AT AUGUSTA August, 1884 (Courtesy of Raymond Fogler Library Special Collections)

During the business depression of the late 1880's leadership of the band changed hands frequently. For part of 1887, C. E. Wilson was leader; then M. H. Andrews, A. D. Harlow, E. C. Adams, and perhaps others for short times between brief episodes of Hall's tutelage.

Prominent Bangor dentist and violinist Dr. O. E. Wasgatt led the Bangor Band during the portion of 1893 prior to Hall's reelection as leader for 1893-4. Wasgatt's father, Dr. E. T.

Wasgatt was also a dentist who had played the cello in Andrews' Orchestra at the time Hall first arrived in Bangor. In 1884 when Dr. Emery T. Wasgatt was injured, "young master Oscar Wasgatt" played an accomplished violin solo at the benefit concert for his convalescence.[28] Nine years later, and by then a busy dentist, Dr. O. E. Wasgatt was one of the Bangor musicians that Hall engaged for special occasions in Waterville. At the turn of the century he came to play at Hall's concerts for the Colby commencements. He was concertmaster of the Maine Festival Orchestra at the time that Hall was solo cornet.

Hall was again named conductor of the Bangor Band in 1893, although city directories and advertisements for Waterville, as well as newspaper accounts of his activities with the Waterville Military Band, indicate that he lived, taught, and also conducted in Waterville at that time. He accomplished both by commuting by railroad. While on the train he composed and copied parts, his pockets often stuffed with the music he was working on. More than merely a peripatetic music teacher, he was a prototype for the modern day orchestral conductors who hold simultaneous music directorships with orchestras on opposite sides of the country, or even on several different continents at once, and spend their time on an airliner preparing music for the next engagement.

Bangor City Directories for the years from 1882 through the 1890's provide other evidence that Hall's time in Bangor was sporadic rather than eight solid years. The only Bangor City Directory in which R. B. Hall appears is the 1884 issue, listing "Hall, R. B., Musician, Bds (boards) American House." The American House was a large hotel situated at the corner of Harlow and Central streets. It advertised "First Class Accommodations" for $2.00 a night; also "Free Coaches to and from all Boats and Trains." The American House would have been convenient to the Bangor Band's office, which was at 58 Main Street.

The same directory (1884) lists the Bangor Band as "Bangor Military Band," which is typical of Hall's style, and names R. B. Hall as conductor. In no other issues of the Bangor City Directory is Hall listed as a resident, or mentioned as conductor of the Bangor Band. The 1885 directory lists J. M. Mullaly as director of the band, and for the remainder of the 1880's and until 1897 no leader is named in the listing or the advertisement.

In spite of the fact that band records name Hall as conductor off and on for much of the decade, and journalistic biographies would have him spending eight years in Bangor, his style was that of a transient. Even though he received frequent mention in the newspapers, he did not place Bangor adver-

tisements, as he did in other locations where he conducted. He did, however have many private pupils, and many friends in Bangor. He "was on hand for all occasions," as Dr. Maxfield told newsman John Fuller. "He was a familiar sight, short, moustached, walking with a limp....'[29] Here again is another mention of his limp, the same limp that had plagued Hall from childhood, and was to cut short his marching duties in Albany.

This transient style, lack of advertising, and lack of permanent address is in particular contrast to Hall's time in Albany, where he was listed in the directory and also advertised there, although he lived in Albany only a scant six months. He also advertised at least twice a week in the Albany evening paper as leader of the local band. During his years in Waterville, he was listed in the directory every time it was published, advertised in the directory as a teacher and also advertised the band with himself as leader.[30]

In spite of his strong association with Bangor and the Bangor Band, Hall was destined to have an even stronger association with Waterville, where he spent fifteen years and reached the epitome of his career. During all of his time in Waterville, Hall continued to appear frequently in Bangor as a soloist, or with various dance orchestras. In 1893-4, the very midst of his Waterville years (although a year in which the Waterville Military Band was not being very well funded) R. B. Hall returned to Bangor, once again to lead the Bangor Band. This time he was definitely a transient, and lived in Waterville, where he continued to make his career.

It was in Bangor, however, that Hall had begun composing in earnest, and this was the arena of his activities that, more than his leadership of any band or his performance in any orchestra, was to achieve his greatest fame, securing his memory for future generations. Hall's first published march was entitled *M.H.A.* in honor of Melville H. Andrews. It was published in 1887 by W. H. Cundy in Boston, though Hall was believed to have written it in 1884. Later Varney recalled having been told by Hall that he had sold it to Mace Gay for five dollars.[31] That may, however, have been one of the other marches from this same era confused with *M.H.A.* in the retelling. Whether he sold it to Cundy for that amount or whether that was a reflection on his dealings with Gay is impossible to determine, but in any event Hall sold the march rather cheaply.

Also originating about the same time was Hall's march *Lodoeska* in honor of his mother, Virginia Lodoeska (Browne) Hall. A cheerful six-eight march, it was published in 1889 by Mace Gay, though Hall had composed it five years earlier, in 1884 at the age of 25. Several of Hall's early marches came out in the same year, 1889, a fact that makes it seem that a publishing breakthrough opened the way for the release of a backlog of Hall's compositions. He had been working at composing for several years as he taught lessons, led the band, played in Andrews' Orchestra, and instructed or coached other bands in Cherryfield, Belfast, Garland, Newport, and elsewhere.

In one year, 1889, Mace Gay published *Kineo*, dedicated to the newly reconstructed resort hotel on Moosehead Lake where Hall often played; *Randolph*, dedicated to the town of Randolph, Maine, which was incorporated as a town distinct from the neighboring town of Pittston in 1887; and *General Mitchell,* dedicated to General Henry L. Mitchell, a prominent Bangor attorney who helped rebuild the Bangor Band. *Stella Polka,* perhaps the most difficult cornet solo written by Hall, was also released that same year by Mace Gay. It was dedicated to Miss Stella Hunter.

NOTES

1 NA#2228.011. Also NA#2261.021-023, .034-035.

2 Thomas C. Bardwell, Sr., "The New England March King" *Fanfare Magazine 1:10 (1977), 28.*

3 *Bangor* [Maine] *Daily Commercial*, 17 April 1884, 4.

4 Some of these early pieces are among the material that was collected by Ralph Gould and now is archived at the Bagaduce Music Lending Library in Blue Hill, Maine. Partial scores to some strains of the early "R.C.B." marches are included, but these are untitled, or titled differently.

5 *BDC*, 27 May 1884, 4.

6 *BDC*, 28 May 1884, 1.

7 *BDC*, 28 May 1884, 4.

8 *BDC*, 16 July 1894.

9 *BDC*, 2 July 1884, 1.

10 *BDC*, 5 July 1884, 4.

11 *BDC*, 11 July 1884, 4.

12 A photocopy of the original letter in Andrews' hand on Oceanic Hotel stationery can be seen at the Bagaduce Music Lending Library, Blue Hill, Maine, Hall collection, folder 8.

13 *BDC*, 11 July 1884, 4.

14 Ibid.

15 Ibid.

16 *BDC*, 12 July 1884, 4.

17 *BDC*, 29 July 1884, 4.

18 *BDC*, 31 July 1884, 1.

19 Ralph Gould, "R. B. Hall—Maine's Music Man," *Down East,* October 1967, 30-33.

20 I made such an arrangement for the Bangor Band to perform at the 1985 R. B. Hall Day. It was included in the "State Of Maine" collection of Hall's marches reissued by the late Bangor physician James D. Clement, who also played tuba in the Bangor Band.

21 R. B. Hall, *Kineo March*, (Brockton, MA: Mace Gay, 1889), m. 21-38.

22 George Thornton Edwards, *Music and Musicians of Maine,* (Portland, Maine: The Southworth Press, 1928), 398-399.

23 *BDC*, 30 July 1884, 4.

24 *BDC*, 11 August 1884, 4.

25 *BDC*, 9 August 1884, 4.

26 The Bangor Band library is currently located in an upstairs room at Bangor Parks and Recreation, 647 Main Street, Bangor, Maine. Access can be arranged by contacting a band officer.

27 *Crean's March* was never published. It is distinct from all Hall's other marches, in that the parts of this march were not reworked and published under another title. A photocopy of the manuscript is in the Bangor Band's library.

28 *BDC*, 6 June 1884.

29 John Fuller, op. cit.

30 He did not advertise the band in the newspaper. He did not need to. Instead, in Waterville the local paper (The *Waterville Mail*) took it upon itself to announce Hall's concerts, and to plead with the public to underwrite the summer concert series.

31 NA#2261.032-033.

CHAPTER FOUR
TRANSITION FROM BANGOR TO WATERVILLE
(1890-1891)

Of the many places where Hall lived and worked, the central Maine city of Waterville bears the strongest association with his life. Here he lived the longest, composed the majority of his mature works, and directed the town band and orchestra which became known as Hall's Band and Hall's Orchestra. Here he settled, taught, married, joined a men's club, and lived until his final illness at age 48 took him to his mother's home in Portland for the last six months of his life.

Some existing short biographies indicate that Hall began his work in Waterville in 1890, but a close inspection of the local papers indicates that the Waterville period in Hall's career did not actually begin until the late winter of 1891. His custom of titling his marches for persons, events, or organizations with which he was associated reflects this as well. For the thirty-two-year-old Hall, 1890 was a year of impermanence in which he traveled over much of the state, and directed many different bands. Perhaps his 1890 march, *Flirtation*, was titled in this state of mind.

THE TRANSITIONAL YEAR (1890)

It is not certain where Hall had his residence for much of 1890, if indeed he had a permanent residence in any city that year. The Bangor city directory does not list or mention him in that year. The 1890 census for Maine was destroyed in a fire, so it cannot be consulted. Although no city directories for 1890 or '91 are available to establish Hall's residence in Waterville, when he first moved to Waterville in 1891 the newspapers gave the fact plenty of attention.

For the previous eight years in Bangor, dance and theater work with Andrews' Orchestra had been the mainstay of Hall's livelihood. During 1890, M. H. Andrews gave up night work with his orchestra in order to found his music store, Andrews' Music House; the orchestra soon disbanded. The Bangor News reported Hall playing a solo with Andrews' Orchestra in February, 1890,[1] but by June, M. H. Andrews was in Boston[2] and Hall was entirely out of the news as far as the Bangor Band was concerned.[3] Only occasional orchestra work was reported.[4] The following autumn, with no orchestra work in Bangor, Hall turned to band instructing in several cities simultaneously, as he cast about for a permanent position.

Hall's increasing status with bands around the state is borne out by his march titles for 1890. Dates on Hall's published marches can sometimes be taken as an indication as to when certain events or associations alluded to in the titles touched his life, but can also be misleading. Occasionally his marches were written, titled and published in the same year. More often there was a lag of a year or even several between completion and publication. Of the eight marches that Hall published in 1890 some may well have been newly written, but many were marches that had been played in their manuscript versions for several previous years.

In 1890 his marches included titles related to Bangor, Gardiner, and Lewiston, but not Waterville. These marches are: *G.M.B.*, for the Gardiner Military Band; *L.B.B.*, for the Lewiston Brigade Band; *Kennebec*, for a newly launched excursion steamer that plied the Kennebec River; *Adjutant Bridge*, for Adjutant Olin D. Bridge of Bangor's Company G, premiered in 1884; *Col. Brett*, for Col. Victor L. Brett of the Second Regiment in Lewiston; *Algerine*, which bore

the manuscript title "The Comical Indian" and is a reworking of part of one of the early "R.C.B." marches; *Bangor*, premiered in 1884 under the original title "Col. Perkins"; and *Flirtation*, which may have characterized the state of Hall's career in that year. No one publisher was favored; Mace Gay, Oliver Ditson, Jean Missud, and W. H. Cundy each contributed to Hall's output. Perhaps Hall's "flirtation" was as much with various publishers as with various bands.

In 1890 Hall was listed as director of the American Cadet Band in Portland;[5] was said to be director of Chandler's Band, also in Portland;[6] and entitled marches for the Lewiston Brigade Band and Gardiner Military Band, which is taken by many to indicate a connection with, or even leadership of, these bands as well.

Insofar as published march titles can be taken to imply a connection with the group included in the title, Hall's composition list for 1891 might reflect his activities of 1890. His 1891 publications include *Chandler's* and *Chilcothian*, each formally dedicated to the eponymous organization. This has led to the assumption that Hall directed Chandler's Band in Portland during the previous year. He may well have spent some time with Chandler's Band as an instructor, although the band's official history does not mention it.

Some confusion has always existed between the American Cadet Band and Chandler's band, because both were founded and directed by men named Chandler. Daniel H. Chandler had founded Chandler's band from the previously existing Old Portland Band in 1873. His son William E. Chandler founded the American Cadet Band in 1886, which took up the regalia of the Old Portland Cadets as their first uniform. Both D. H. and W. E. Chandler taught and coached numerous other bands throughout the state.[7] Coincidentally, Daniel H. Chandler had been the first teacher of the band in Richmond, in 1854, in which Hall's father, Nathaniel Hall later played cornet, and which was the progenitor of the Richmond Cornet Band, that R. B. Hall was later to lead.[8]

Whether or not Hall actually taught or led Chandler's band at this time, the dedication of his march Chandler's is definite. The first printing of the march by Mace Gay in 1891 bears the inscription: "Respectfully dedicated to 'Chandler's Band' of Portland, Me." at the top of the Solo Cornet part.

The other 1891 title, *Chilcothian*, bears the formal dedication: "Respectfully dedicated to the 'Chilcothians' Bangor, Maine." The Chilcothians were a very successful and long-lived young women's drill team organized by and named for their coach, Langdon S. Chilcott.[9] Chilcott was the author of *Templar*

EXAMPLE 2. March Chilcothian, by R. B. Hall. Solo Cornet part.[11]

Tactics and Manual, a slim volume containing instructions for marching, forming drill squads, and providing music for drum signals, bugle signals and various marching cadences.[10] Hall's march itself contains drum ruffles and bugle signals like those in Chilcott's book, and also "Annie Laurie," a tune which was immensely popular at that time, included presumably in deference to the gender of the marchers.

The trio of Chilcothian consists of a hymn-like melody which Hall credited to the S. Brainard's Sons Co., but which is otherwise unidentified.[12] The Chilcothians had been very active in Bangor during 1890, with Bangor educator Mary E. Snow as their advisor, and Captain Chilcott as their drill instructor.[13]

BANDS IN WATERVILLE AT THE TIME OF HALL'S ARRIVAL.

Discussions of Hall's involvement in Waterville almost invariably start with a reference to the development of a band there by Horatio Fales, a band which later became Hall's Waterville Military Band. The impression for the present-day reader is that this was the beginning of band music in Waterville, though such is not the truth. Actually there had been an active band scene in Waterville since shortly after the Civil War, with several small groups of bandsmen combining and recombining to fill the demand for outdoor music in the area. Formed in 1882, the Union Band of Waterville had considerable cross-membership with the newly formed Waterville "City" Band, as news photos of the two groups show.[14] The Union Band, "City" Band, and Fairfield Band were each trying to form a combination which could result in a successful band to fill the need for outdoor music and compete with the nearby Oakland Band, which was already well established and served the summer community.

The City Band (also called the Waterville Band) was organized in Waterville during 1890 by a group of men headed up by Horatio Fales, a highly-esteemed Waterville music teacher. Although in Waterville he was primarily an orchestra leader and violinist, Fales had played the keyed bugle in the Boston Brass Band during the 1830s and '40s under direction of the famed Ned Kendall. Later he was co-leader of Flagg and Fales Quadrille Band, also of Boston, before coming to Waterville in the 1860s. In Waterville he led a number of bands and orchestras over the years, and traveled with them throughout the state. Eventually he favored orchestra work over band work, and as his age advanced he concentrated on the teaching of violin and orchestral strings. He coached the ladies orchestra in Waterville, and eventually two of his pupils, the Leahy sisters, formed an orchestra which became quite famous in the years after 1900. In 1890, Fales was 71 years old when he suggested to Hall that he could find favorable conditions in Waterville.[15]

The Union Band (of Waterville—many other towns also had a "Union Band") garnered most of the news in the spring of 1890, and played the "national airs" for the 1890 memorial day celebration.[16] Soon, however, news shifted to the "Waterville Band" as their excursions were announced in the paper.[17] There had been no band concert on the Fourth of July, and the *Mail* reported that: "The fourth was observed very quietly in town....quite a few went to Portland."[18] A few bandsmen had other ideas, however, and had a midnight parade. Again according to the *Mail:* "The 'devil's band' paraded from 12:01 AM 'till daylight, and serenaded a few of the most prominent citizens."[19]

Meanwhile a band had started in Fairfield, the neighboring community just to the north of Waterville. Though they were just forming, they were reported as "practicing diligently," and were planning a series of open air concerts.[20] The Fairfield Band, for all its good beginnings, did not last long, and by the following winter, the Waterville band was playing at the Fairfield skating rink two nights a week.[21] As time went on, many of the Waterville band members actually resided in Fairfield.

By the time R. B. Hall arrived in Waterville in February of 1891 there was a great deal of interest in developing a quality band for Waterville. The existing bands would provide the necessary members to get started, but organization, leadership and funding would be necessary to shape them into a band of which the city could be proud. Hall was just the kind of leader that was needed, and over the next fifteen years he would mold the Waterville Band into an exemplary organization.

HALL'S FIRST YEAR IN WATERVILLE (1891)

Although the band scene was already important and newsworthy in Waterville, once Hall arrived in the city the level of attention paid to the band increased. From occasional mentions of band doings, a call for a summer concert series emerged. The *Waterville Mail*, a weekly Republican paper, carried news of the developments on its generally gossipy local page. Occasional editorials underscored the *Mail's* support for the idea of summer concerts.[22]

The fact that the band that ultimately became the Waterville Military Band was begun by Horatio Fales, and was later renamed by Hall, is well-documented by following the events of 1891 in the Waterville Mail. Practically every week that year some item relevant to the band scene in Waterville, or to Hall's biography, was printed. On February 20 the following short notice appeared in the "local matters" section:

Prof. R.B. Hall, the cornetist, has taken up his abode in this city for the present.[23]

This fixes the date of Hall's arrival in Waterville, and eliminates the general assumption that he had moved sometime in 1890. Whether he had already been invited to lead the band, as Gould stated in his piece for *Down East*,[24] is unknown, but events as they unfold in the spring seem to suggest that his leadership of the band developed over the spring and summer of 1891, and that his livelihood was initially made by playing in an orchestra. Beth Haines, the daughter of William D. Haines, a Dexter, Maine, composer and bandmaster who was a Hall disciple and leader of the Waterville Military Band after Hall's death until 1926, wrote an authoritative piece on the history of bands in Waterville for the *Sentinel* in 1952. In it she indicates that Fales was influential in bringing Hall to Waterville.[25]

As he had in Bangor, Hall played with a local orchestra. Dinsmore's Orchestra in Waterville filled the place in Hall's initial activity there that Andrews' Orchestra had during his Bangor years. It supplied the theater and dance engagements that complemented band work and teaching to make a full-time musician's life. As had been the case in Bangor, Hall's cornet solos made a big impression on the public, and the newspaper reported his engagements and solos practically every week. Thus, the following announcement of a ball for the Sons of Veterans from March 13:

The concert and ball to be given on the evening of March 20 by Garfield Camp, S. of V. promises to be an affair of much interest. Dinsmore's orchestra of 5 pieces with R. B. Hall as Cornet soloist and Miss Marion Howard, soprano, and Mr. W. C. Philbrook, tenor.[sic] [26]

This brief announcement shows Dinsmore's orchestra to be a small orchestra indeed. Then, as now, having an ensemble of only five pieces meant the ability to play many more commercial engagements than a larger unit could hope to obtain. It also shows that Hall was in contact with W. C. Philbrook from his earliest time in Waterville.

Warren C. Philbrook (1857-1933) was a prominent Waterville attorney, a Colby '82 graduate who later became assistant state attorney general, then attorney general, mayor of Waterville, state senator, and eventually an associate justice of the Maine Supreme Court. In addition, he was an active amateur musician, a tenor who sang frequently with excellent reviews, and who trained the chorus for various community musicals and benefits. As a tenor, he was to sing with Hall's band and orchestra occasionally.

As a politician Philbrook was to speak at many of the civic functions for which Hall was to lead the band during the next fifteen years. His law offices were at 105 Main Street, just down the block from the headquarters of the Waterville Military Band at 93 Main Street. Furthermore, in addition to being both a Mason and an Odd Fellow, Philbrook was an important member of the Canabas Club, of which Hall was later to become a member. Seldom did a week go by without some item about Philbrook appearing in the news. Hall was to be in frequent contact with him throughout his entire Waterville career.

As had been the case in Bangor, Hall's association with the band began soon after his arrival. An item in the Waterville *Mail* for March 20, one month after the notice of his arrival in the city, indicates that he will be engaged to teach the band.

It is hoped and expected that the excellent material now composing the City Band will, under the instruction of Prof. R. B. Hall, develop into an organization second to none of its kind in this part of the state. But it requires time and expense on the part of the boys which we trust our citizens will appreciate. Some open air concerts during the spring and summer nights will be the proper thing. [27]

The *Mail* is pursuing the idea of summer open air concerts, which were popular at the time, but which were not yet available in Waterville. Hall is mentioned as instructor, but not yet band leader. The time for rehearsal and practice was an issue then, even as it is now. The expense of operating a band was hinted at, and throughout the years this became a theme in the *Mail,* as the band struggled for funds to continue, to engage Hall as leader, and to provide summer concerts.

The following week, the first of Hall's many Waterville compositions was dedicated and announced in the paper. It was the march *Waterville*.

The announcement in the newspaper praised its heavy and showy style.

We learn that Prof. R. B. Hall dedicates his latest march to the city of Waterville. It will be published in the course of a few weeks, and cannot fail to become a favorite with the full military bands that want a heavy and at the same time a showy march. [29]

The march *Waterville* was copyrighted by Mace Gay in 1892, and did indeed become a favorite. This brief announcement fixes the date of its completion by Hall as March of 1891, and its position as the first march completed after he moved to Waterville. Interestingly, it does not bear a formal dedication to the city on the printed parts, though the newspaper piece leaves no doubt that Hall

EXAMPLE 3. *Waterville March, by R. B. Hall. Solo Cornet part.*[28]

intended the title to bear a dedicatory sentiment.

Elsewhere in the same issue was a short item concerning the reorganization of the band:

The city band held a meeting for reorganization last evening, and voted to secure the services of Prof. Hall as instructor until the first of May, at which time they will give him a benefit concert. They will then try to secure his services for a longer time, and citizens will be asked to aid by contributing for a series of open air concerts.[30]

Little did they realize then, that R. B. Hall would be their leader for the next fifteen years. Once again, money was an issue in whether there would be summer concerts, and this was far from the last time that the *Mail* would mention money for the band. The benefit concert did not actually take place until May 26, but when it did it was a huge success. The poster for the "Grand Benefit Concert" including the long, elaborate program with many soloists, appears in Figure 1.

A short review appeared in the next Friday's paper.

The concert given by the Waterville Military Band, Tuesday evening, for the benefit of Prof. R. B. Hall, was well attended, considering the state of the weather, and was thoroughly enjoyed by all. The band was assisted by Mrs. Helen Winslow Potter and Mr. Boardman of Bangor, and Mr. W. C. Philbrook of this city, each of whom received hearty

FIGURE 1: *Grand Benefit Concert poster, May 26, 1891. (Courtesy of Bagaduce Music Lending Library, Blue Hill, Maine)*

encores. The Band played some very pleasing selections and showed that it is a musical organization of much promise. It is to be hoped that a series of outdoor concerts can be arranged for by the band for the summer months.[31]

This was the first use in the newspaper of the name "Waterville Military Band." The fact that the band had been renamed probably reflects Hall's decision to stay on as leader. The review is unusually lengthy for the Waterville *Mail*, and the concert must have been considered very special to get that much attention. It is noteworthy that Hall enlisted the aid of two Bangor vocalists, as well as W. C. Philbrook, in order to make sure the concert was a considerable attraction.

Meanwhile, the annual Canton Halifax ball had taken place on April 21. That year the prestigious event did not include Hall in the orchestra, for Pullen's orchestra had been engaged, and Hall was busy that spring with Dinsmore's Orchestra.[32] By the following year this would not be the case. Hall's presence would be indispensable to the prestigious event and he would be engaged to play with Pullen's Orchestra.[33]

Hall did perform at a different and perhaps even more prestigious affair that spring, however. The Canabas Club gave a huge ball in its newly redecorated four story building.

The flowers and decorations were said to be the most elaborate yet seen in the city. The sumptuous refreshments were described in detail. The featured entertainment was a concert in the early part of the evening by Dinsmore's Orchestra with R. B. Hall as cornet soloist, followed by a dance which did not end until 12:30 a.m. Billiards and whist were provided for those who did not wish to dance.

The membership list of the Canabas Club was given, and it included about thirty of the most prominent lawyers, politicians, doctors, and financial executives in Waterville. W. C. Philbrook was prominent among them, as were horseman Appleton Webb, bank owner F. C. Thayer, financier Frank Redington, and physician Dr. J. F. Hill. These club members and others became the group that was, nine years later, to incorporate to support the Waterville Military Band. The long guest list included the most influential people in Maine, and two columns of the newspaper were devoted to what the ladies wore.[34] Hall could not have appeared before a more respected and influential audience. At that time he probably did not even dream that he would actually become a member of the prestigious Canabas club twelve years later.

Not to be outdone, the Waterville Masonic lodge dedicated and opened its brand-new four story building in June. Details of the architecture and decorations of this huge new building, to be known as the Masonic Block, had been published in the news all spring. The Masonic chambers themselves were said to be the most elaborate and artistic of any north of Boston at that time. Festivities were scheduled for the entire weekend. The consecration ceremony was followed by a dedication which included a Friday night reception and ball which lasted until midnight, and for which Hall played. W. C. Philbrook was master of ceremonies, and the guest list included Masonic and political dignitaries from the entire state. The next day began with a parade at 9:00 a.m. with R. B. Hall and the Waterville Military Band leading the way. This was an event for the whole city, as the big fancy parade wound its way through much of Waterville in a long parade route. In addition to Hall's Band, the Palestine Commandery Band of Belfast also paraded and performed.[35]

That was not the only activity for Hall's band that day. The Colby baseball team had been to Brunswick to play the Bowdoin team, and on their return rode through town with a rousing reception. The Waterville Military Band had been engaged for the occasion, and according to the Mail, there was a large crowd.[36]

The following Thursday the Waterville Military Band gave the first of the outdoor concerts which were to become its tradition. Once again the paper commented on the need for a public subscription to fund the band for these open air concerts.[37]

During the ensuing month, the Waterville Military Band was busy with excursions, and played its outdoor concerts from the steps of the various hotels in the city; one week the Elmwood, the next, the Bayview, and so forth as if casting about for a suitable location. On July 16, 1891 they hit upon a location which was to become the customary site for the band's outdoor concerts in the coming years. For the first time they played in Monument Park, on the west side of Elm Street, between Park Street and Coburn Classical Institute. This area had been called Monument Park, and was generally known by that name, even though it was not officially so designated until April, 1894.[38] This was to become the usual site for the band's outdoor concerts. The *Mail* published an editorial on the subject the following Friday:

A GOOD CHOICE

The Military Band selected an excellent location, in Monument Park for its Thursday evening concert. The Park is just the place for such events. To be sure, some persons may now and then stray from the gravel walks upon the grass, but if there is any better purpose to which the lawn of the park can be put that to the pleasure of citizens, we fail to think of it. The park is a thing of beauty and should be kept as such, but it ought to be above all else a spot to cater to the innocent enjoyment of "the people."[39]

This location met with such favor and acceptance that within two weeks it was considered "usual" as the following item indicates:

The usual band concert was given in the park, near the residence of Rev. J. L. Seward, Thursday evening. After the programme, the musicians and others were tendered an informal reception at Mr. Seward's house, where they enjoyed a social hour, and partook of refreshments including coffee, cake, and ice cream.[40]

The fact that the newspaper reported the reception as well as the concert indicates how closely the affairs of the band were followed, and how much it was appreciated.

Band music was important at that time, and people would travel to hear it. When Gilmore's band had appeared in Portland, a special excursion train took passengers from Bangor, Skowhegan, and Waterville directly to the concerts.[41] One popular destination was Maranacook Lake, just west of Augusta, where Sunday sacred concerts were a frequent summertime feature. Figure 2 is a poster advertising one such concert with the Waterville Military Band.

Hall's band often played these sacred concerts at Maranacook, but so did a number of other bands including the Bangor Band, the Oakland Band, Chandler's Band, and others from around the state. Throughout the 1870's and 80's, and less frequently in the 1890's, a band festival was held there which drew the best of Maine's many town bands and large crowds of spectators for the concerts and contests. Early in his career Hall had engaged in a cornet duel there, in which he was bested by Charles Lyndall, a fine player who was, however, related to the judges. Hall's supporters, knowing that the contest was rigged, bought him a better cornet than the one offered as a prize.[42]

An item in the Waterville *Mail* in August, 1891, indicates that 57 Waterville people traveled to Maranacook to hear the Bangor Band's sacred concert on Sunday, August 9.[43] In the ensuing seasons Hall's Waterville Military Band was also frequently to appear at these Sunday sacred concerts as well as numerous other excursions to Maranacook.

As it had been in his youth and was so often to be in the future, Hall's health was an issue for the Waterville Military Band and its public even as early as 1891. The Waterville *Mail* reported any

"MUSIC IN THE WOODS"
GRAND
CONCERT
AT
Lake Maranacook
ON
SUNDAY, JULY 24
BY THE
WATERVILLE MILITARY BAND

PROGRAMME.

MARCH, "Waterville,"	R: B. Hall.	VOCAL SCHOTTISCHE, "Laugh! Oh Coons,"	
OVERTURE, "Bohemian Girl,"	Balfe		Wheeler.
CONCERT VALSE, "Summer Nights,"	Stone.	OVERTURE, "Lustpiel."	Keler Bela.
CORNET SOLO, "Flocktonian,"	Casey.	SPANISH VALSE, "Aphrodite,"	Jaxome.
R. B. HALL.		BARITONE SOLO, "Serenade,"	Luscomb.
POTPOURRI, "Operatic Airs,"	Beyer.		J. E. SAWYER.
SERENADE, "Harvest Moon,"	Ripley.	GALOP, "Bacchanal,"	Rollinson.
R. B. HALL, Soloist and Conductor.			

AN EXCELLENT DINNER WILL BE SERVED ON THE GROUNDS

FINE OPPORTUNITIES FOR
ROWING AND STEAMBOATING
ON THIS
MOST BEAUTIFUL OF MAINE LAKES
AMPLE SHELTER IN CASE OF RAIN.

The MAINE CENTRAL R. R.

Offers Special Trains and Fares as follows :

	A. M.	FARE		A. M.	FARE
Portland, de	8.45	$1.00	Monmouth	10.50	.45
Woodfords	8.50	1.00	Annabessacook	10.56	.40
Westbrook Junc.	8.55	1.00	Winthrop	11.03	.25
Falmouth	9.02	1.00	Maranacook, ar	11.10	
Cumberland Junc.	9.09	1.00	Skowhegan, de	9.20	$1.00
Walnut Hill	9.24	1.00	Pishon's Ferry	9 36	1.00
Gray	9.35	1.00	Shawmut	9.44	.95
New Gloucester	9.44	1.00	Fairfield	9.53	.85
Rowe's	0.49	.75	Waterville	10.05	.75
Danville Junc.	9.54	.75	Oakland	10.18	.65
Auburn	10.06	.75	North Belgrade	10.26	.55
Lewiston	10.15	.75	Belgrade	10.36	.45
Greene	10.29	.75	Readfield	10.52	.25
Leeds Junc.	10.40	.60	Maranacook, ar	11.00	

Returning---Specials will leave the Lake for all points at 5.00 p. m., arriving Portland at 7.15 p. m., Skowhegan at 6.40 p. m.

F. E. BOOTHBY, G.P.&T.A

PAYSON TUCKER, V.P.&GEN'L MANAGER

FIGURE 2. Concert Poster, July 24, 1891. (Courtesy Bagaduce Music Lending Library, Blue Hill, Maine)

change in Hall's health that affected the band's schedule. Thus the following:

The regular band concert for Tuesday evening was postponed on account of the illness of band leader Hall. No concert will be given this week. The band is doing lots of practicing for the music they will give on the day of the Northport excursion.[44]

By the following week Hall's health had returned sufficiently that the Mail noted the customary concert with the usual crowd on Thursday night. The story on the excursion to Northport mentioned 260 people from Waterville, joining others already on the train.[45] Northport is a community on the shore of Penobscot Bay, midway between Belfast and Lincolnville. Summer residents and excursionists alike went there for clam and lobster bakes on the shore at Saturday Cove, and dancing at the pavilion at Bayside.[46] No wonder the band had been practicing.

Once again in late August, the Mail ran a fairly long editorial piece on the band, stressing the need for more general financial support for the summer concerts.

Our citizens have greatly enjoyed the open air concerts by the Waterville Military Band during the summer months and have contributed liberally to the financial support of the organization. The canvass for subscriptions has not been conducted very thoroughly and the expenses of the band have been quite large for the new music and other necessary items. The management at a recent meeting decided to allow the public to give a more general testimonial of the appreciation which is felt for the efforts of Mr. Hall and his fellow musicians in supporting a first-class band in the city, and some time in October a fair to continue three days will be held at city hall for the benefit of the organization. Good entertainment will be furnished, and all will have an opportunity to contribute slightly towards an object well worthy of support.[47]

As usual, the financial condition of the band needed bolstering, but it was not until the following spring, when preparations for the forthcoming season necessitated it, that the fair actually took place. When it did, it was a huge success with the public, although not raising as much money as had been hoped.

The remainder of August was marked by an excursion to Kineo on which the entire band went, and further experimentation with the location for Waterville city concerts. Concerts were also given in Fairfield during September. The final band concert for the season was on the 24th of September, and the Mail ran a short and very laudatory review the next day, praising the band's improvement and Hall's conducting. Through the fall little news of the band was published, and the impression is that a period of dormancy was expected. News of Hall's cornet solos and work by Dinsmore's and Haley's orchestras shows that musical work shifted more strongly to dances and theatrical shows once the outdoor season was over.

The Waterville Military Band gave a concert and ball at city hall on Thanksgiving Day evening, and then in December the [Waterville] Union Band and the Waterville Military Band joined forces. According to the local news in the *Mail*:

By an almost unanimous vote of the members of the Waterville Military Band and the Union Band, the two organizations are to be consolidated in the near future. Prof. R. B. Hall will continue as the leader and instructor of the new band.[48]

This action by the Union band, which was reported as "almost unanimous," was evidently not undisputed. Some of the Union band's members seemed to feel there was room in the local market for two bands to compete. It was retracted in the newspaper a month later, in a short notice which read as follows:

The managers of the Union Band wish the MAIL to announce that the report that the organization has disbanded is without foundation. It is still in the field and open to engagements.[49]

Despite the protestations of its managers, the Union Band disappeared from the scene and was never heard from again. The majority who joined Hall's band had enlisted in the band which would soon succeed and predominate.

Through the winter months, there was once again little band news, orchestra work tending to dominate as dances and theatricals commanded people's attention during the cold weather. Hall's popularity as a soloist was such that the paper had to take Lucier's Minstrels (a very popular traveling stage show that played an occasional week-long engagement in Waterville) to task for doing an imitation of R. B. Hall playing the cornet. In spite of complimenting the dancing and costumes in a generally favorable review of the popular show, the editor chided Lucier as follows:

We should advise Mr. Lucier to give up his imitation of Prof. R. B. Hall on the cornet, as it is the poorest thing he does: he is not up to the original in any way.[50]

Generally, during that January and February, about two classy dances or affairs called "sociables" were given each week, and Dinsmore's Orchestra and Hall's solos received frequent mention. A ball usually consisted of twelve to fifteen dances described in advance according to a program, and lasting from about 9:00 p.m. until midnight or 12:30 a.m. If there was no program, but the order of the dances was at the discretion of the band leader (often called the "prompter") or the master of ceremonies, then the affair was described as a "hop." "Sociables" were gatherings at which there was entertainment, often a short concert with solos, and a literary reading. Refreshments were usually served.

The military ball given by Waterville's Company H of the Second Regiment, Maine Volunteer Militia, on February 29 was the first appearance of a hitherto unheard of group: the Waterville Military Band Orchestra. Though no mention was made of its membership, its venues as time went on made it obvious that this was a group drawn from the Waterville Military Band for the purpose of playing dance engagements. Hall could thus book dances without having to go through one of the established orchestra leaders, and the reputation of the Waterville Military Band was sufficient to assure a steady supply of inquiries. Over the ensuing years the Waterville Military Band Orchestra

(sometimes somewhat quizzically shortened simply to "Band Orchestra") obtained an ever-increasing share of the dance work whenever Hall was in town and active.

It is likely that the inception of the "Band Orchestra" was a fortuitous result of the fact that another large ball was offered on the same night as the military ball, and Dinsmore's Orchestra couldn't be in two places at once. The "Leap Year's Ball," with Dinsmore's small orchestra, featured complete role reversal. The young ladies planned and sponsored the affair, invited the young men, picked them up, escorted them to the ball, asked them to dance, treated them to refreshments, and returned them home at the end of the evening. This was unusual enough in 1892 to get a good deal of attention from the newspaper. Hall's first full year in Waterville had included a reorganization and renaming of the City Band, the establishment of a summer concert series, the establishment of a reputation for excellence which was to be enhanced in the future, the founding of the Waterville Military Band Orchestra, and the dedication of his march Waterville. His next year was to begin with a fund raising effort.

NOTES

[1] *Bangor* [Maine] *News*, 21 February 1890.

[2] *Bangor* [Maine] *Daily Commercial*, 23 June 1890, 1. (Hereafter *BDC).*

[3] *BDC*, 6 June 1890, 3.

[4] *BDC*, 25 June 1890, 3.

[5] Edwards, op. cit., 334.

[6] Letter from USMC Historian Joan Ambrose to Ralph Gould, 20 December 1963. This letter may be seen at Bagaduce Music Lending Library in Blue Hill, Maine (folder 1).

[7] Edwards, op. cit., 333-334.

[8] Fleming, *Richmond on the Kennebec*, 128-129.

[9] Abigail E. Zelz and Marilyn Zoidis, *Woodsmen and Whigs: Historic Images of Bangor,* (Virginia Beach, Virginia: The Donning Co., 1991), 166.

[10] Langdon S. Chilcott, *Templar Tactics and Manual,* (Bangor, Maine: Burr Printing, 1907)

[11] R. B. Hall, *Chilcothian,* (Brockton, Massachusetts: Mace Gay, 1891).

[12] The passage is marked "Used by premission of the S. Brainard's Sons Co."

[13] *BDC*, 23, 24, 25 June 1890.

[14] *WS*, 10 July 1952, supplement.

[15] *WS*, 19 September 1905. Material on Fales is all taken from a lengthy career retrospective published as a feature on this date.

[16] W*M*, 6 June 1890.

[17] *WM*, 20 June 1890.

[18] *WM*, 18 July 1890.

[19] Ibid.

[20] Ibid.

[21] *WM*, 23 January 1891.

[22] The *Waterville Sentinel,* a Democratic weekly (semi-weekly during some of these years) was Waterville's other paper. Unfortunately, no issues were preserved or microfilmed for the years prior to 1904, at which time the *Sentinel* became a daily, and began keeping a permanent collection of back issues.

[23] *WM*, 20 February 1891.

[24] Ralph Gould, "R. B. Hall - Maine's Music Man" *Down East*, October 1967, 30.

[25] *Waterville* [Maine] *Sentinel*, 10 July 1952. (Hereafter *WS*).

[26] *WM*, 13 March 1891.

[27] *WM*, 20 March 1891.

[28] R. B. Hall, *Waterville March*, (Brockton, Massachusetts: Mace Gay, 1892).

[29] *WM*, 27 March 1891.

[30] id.

[31] *WM*, 29 May 1891.

[32] *WM*, 27 March 1891. *WM*, 24 April 1891.

[33] W*M*, 1 April 1892.

[34] *WM*, 22 May 1891.

[35] *WM*, 12 June 1891.

[36] Ibid.

[37] Ibid.

[38] *WM*, 6 April 1894.

[39] *WM*, 17 July 1891.

[40] *WM*, 31 July 1891.

[41] *WM*, 3 April 1891.

[42] Recollections of Howard Mansir, reported in *Lewiston* [Maine] *Journal*, 15 July 1922.

[43] *WM*, 14 August 1891.

[44] Ibid.

[45] *WM*, 21 August 1891.

[46] There is a summer colony of quaint cottages, and a golf club with a pavilion that gives occasional dances there to this day.

[47] *WM*, 21 August 1891.

[48] *WM*, 4 December 1891.

[49] *WM*, 15 January 1892.

[50] Ibid.

CHAPTER FIVE
ESTABLISHING A PRESENCE IN WATERVILLE
(1892-1894)

After a busy and successful first year in Waterville, Hall began his second year there with an effort to consolidate the gains made by the Waterville Military Band since his arrival. A three-day fund raising fair with different entertainment for each evening was planned for March 15, 16, and 17, 1892. Prior to the fair a fund drive sought contributions. The editors of the *Mail* praised the band as "increasing in efficiency" and the effort as "surely worth the most generous support of the people of this city."[1] A lengthy announcement, written as an editorial rather than a news item, exhorted the band's following to "show their support of this local institution in a substantial way."[2]

In addition to the editorial which sought contributions and support for the band, a news announcement described the event to come.

The three-days fair for the benefit of the Waterville Military Band will open Tuesday night in a grand concert Tuesday night March 15th in which Miss Katherine M. Ricker of Portland, contralto, Mr. Fred A. Given of Lewiston, Violin, soloist Mr. L. B. Cain of Waterville, basso, and Mr. R. B. Hall cornet soloist will all appear. There will also be a fine programme by the full band. It is expected that Miss Blanche Dingley of Lewiston will be pianist for the concert. There will also be fine stage entertainments Wednesday and Thursday nights. The hall will be handsomely

decorated and no pains spared to make the fair a grand success. Season tickets sold at the very low price of 50 cts.[3]

Judging from the announcement this was to be an unusually spectacular event for the city. Concerts in City Hall were common, but lavish decorations and soloists from out of town in addition to a full band concert made this a special attraction; and this was only to be the first of three days. Arrangements had been in progress for weeks, generating a great deal of excitement. News items the following week described a completely sold-out house, with "every available seat secured in City Hall long before the entertainment began." Decorations included "yard upon yard of bunting and the national emblem," and sale of various items in booths positioned around the hall was touted as "destined to swell the money bag of the band."[4]

The program was lengthy and grand. It is worth including here because of the level of achievement which the selections indicate. It was printed as part of the same lengthy news story and demonstrates the attention paid to the band's presentation at the fair.

This was an elaborate program indicating a great deal of rehearsing on the part of the band, and necessary planning to coordinate the soloists. The band selections include *Lustspiel*, which is still frequently played by better bands; and *Les Huguenots*, a difficult and lengthy operatic selection which is seldom played today. The Bangor Band still occasionally performs this piece, playing from hundred-year-old parts that bear Hall's personal rubber stamp reading "please return to R. B. Hall, cornet soloist, Waterville, Maine." Dependent as it is on string sound, *Pizzicato Polka* is now usually left to orchestras (to today's ears a brass staccato just doesn't sound the same) and most of the other pieces are no longer performed.

As with most band programs at this time, at least one plantation or minstrel-style number was offered. The rage for Negro-style music was so strong that such an inclusion was obligatory. Note that *Old Folks at Home*

Part I		
1. Overture, "Lustspiel"	Keler Bela	Waterville Military Band
2. Violin Solo, "Mose" (the celebrated G-string Solo)	Paganini	Mr. Fred A. Given
3. Song, "The Gay Gitana"	Harris	Miss Katherine M. Ricker
4. Cornet Solo, "Air Varie"	Hartmann	Mr. R. B. Hall
5. Bass Solo, "Creole Love Song"	Buck	Mr. L. B. Cain
6. Violin Solo, "Old Folks at Home"		Mr. Given
7. Song, "Love's Sorrow"	Shelley	Miss Ricker
8. Duet for Violin and Horn, "Tittl's Serenade"		Messrs Given and Hall

Part II
(by the Band)

Concert program as printed in the Waterville Mail, 18 March 1892.

was so commonly offered as to not even have a composer credit on the program, as if it were autochthonous folk music. Actually composed by Stephen Foster, it was the subject of a bitter publication dispute, so the authorship may not have been so simple a matter then as we now take it to be.[6]

R. B. Hall was later to try his hand at this idiom himself with his 1900 cakewalk, *The Creole Queen,* and posthumously published *A Georgia Jade*. Among Hall's unpublished juvenilia is a perfectly ordinary plantation song titled "Ah's Got Suffin' On Mah Mind" indicating that this style was not totally for-

March Creole Queen by R. B. Hall. Solo Cornet Part.[58]

eign to his instincts, though he never chose to pursue the idiom once band composing became his regular creative outlet. In any event, the Waterville Military Band's program included one jig tune, the *Watermelon Club,* by the prolific composer and arranger Louis P. Laurendau (1861-1916). Laurendau's original marches and well-respected transcriptions of classics and salon orchestra favorites still grace many summer band programs. His popularly styled pieces, however, such as the then-brand-new *Watermelon Club,* have been long forgotten.

The *Mail* praised the band's performance, indicating that "it has made great strides under Hall's skillful instruction and can now rank among the leading bands of Maine."[7] The work of the soloists was also reviewed favorably. The following evening the featured attraction was an hour-long demonstration of the phonograph, then very new and a curiosity. A dancing demonstration by members of Haley's dance class filled the remainder of the evening.

Thursday's program was devoted to crowd-pleasing attractions. There were some full band selections; an "Irish Jubilee" by Dr. C. H. Haines of Dexter, that was an enormous popular success; Negro songs to banjo accompaniment; and a whistling solo by Miss Nellie Shaw. The fund-raising auction followed, then a grand ball until 2:00 or 3:00 a.m. with more than 80 couples that was described as the "largest dancing party seen in Waterville for years."[8]

This elaborate three-day event turned a tidy profit of about $250 for the band, an amount considered comfortable by the editors of the *Mail.* Even so, according to the editors, additional funds were needed to assure that there would be a summer series. In any case, the affair was acclaimed as a huge success, artistically and financially.

The next major event to capture Hall's attention was the Grand Concert and Ball of Canton Halifax, the Waterville chapter of Patriarchs Militant, which was the uniformed rank of Odd Fellows. On March 31, it followed the band fair by about two weeks. Hall had not played this prestigious event the previous year, but this year he not only played, but was one of the featured attractions. Pullen's Orchestra, based in Augusta, was employed for the evening, as it had been the previous year, but this time it was "Pullen's Full Orchestra assisted by Mr. R. B. Hall with the cornet." The lengthy concert program featured several cornet solos. Hall played Meacham's *American Patrol,* a piece that is still widely played by bands for patriotic functions today.[9] Dancing lasted until 4:00 a.m. No mention of a new march by Hall was made, but later that year Mace Gay published Hall's march *Canton Halifax,* a sprightly six-eight two-step with a delightful folk-like melody in the trio.

EXAMPLE 4. *March Canton Halifax, by R. B. Hall. Solo Cornet part.[10]*

The remainder of the spring of 1892 was comparatively uneventful for Hall and the Waterville Military Band. Dance orchestra work again was the predominant musical employment until good weather for outdoor concerts, parades, and excursions arrived. The Band gave an Easter concert at City Hall, followed by dancing to music by the "Band Orchestra." Dinsmore's Orchestra was busy with dances and kept Hall busy, though he often played with Pullen's or Haley's orchestras as well, not to mention his own Waterville Military Band Orchestra, which was increasingly busy.

The dance orchestra scene in Waterville was filled with tangled alliances that season. Fred Dinsmore, who was a piano tuner and merchant, sold pianos from the facilities of Carlton's Department Store in Waterville. He was associated (in piano retailing) with M. H. Andrews of Bangor.[11] Dinsmore, like Andrews, also taught dancing classes and played the violin. He advertised (as part of his piano sales and tuning advertisements) to provide music for balls, parties, and assemblies of all types, with either a small or large orchestra, or as a solo pianist or fiddler.[12] Just as Andrews had provided Hall's primary orchestra job in Bangor, Dinsmore provided Hall's original orchestra job in Waterville. Prof. Haley, a local dancing teacher, was also a violinist and violin teacher. He played first violin in Hall's "Band Orchestra" and Hall frequently played solo cornet in Haley's Orchestra.[13] Although Haley must have had a first name it was never used in advertisements or news announcements for his musical activities or dance classes. He was simply Prof. Haley.

On April first, 1892, the band announced that it had engaged R. B. Hall for another year as instructor, and also entrusted him with all the affairs of the band.[14] It is interesting that Hall was not considered a member of the band, nor a permanent fixture, nor was he called "conductor" or "director." Instead, the two terms associated with his appointment were "instructor" and "leader." This made Hall not only musical leader but also financial leader and booking agent, a significant expansion of his responsibilities in Waterville, but comparable to the duties he had during his seasons as leader of the Bangor Band.

Soon the Waterville Military Band and the "Band Orchestra" were busier than ever, with the graduation season and the summer concerts closely followed by the excursion season punctuated by social dances and outings for the Patriarchs Militant and The Knights Templar. Gilmore's band came to Portland on May 14, and a special excursion train took passengers from Bangor, Skowhegan, and Waterville to the concert.[15] The Waterville Military Band performed at Maranacook, and in many of the venues to which Hall had taken the Bangor Band in several previous years. Steamboat excursions down the Kennebec were always favorites with the band and the public. With Hall managing the engagements, the band was busy indeed.

A celebration was held for the centennial of the settlement of Waterville by the Redington and Getchell families, who in 1792 had begun the first dam in the Kennebec river at Ticonic falls. A small observance marked the taming of the Kennebec. Plans were begun for the centennial of the incorporation of the city of Waterville in 1802. Hall was to figure prominently in this much larger celebration when it came to pass ten years later.

In addition to *Canton Halifax*, Mace Gay also published in that same year (1892) Hall's *The Sentinel*, dedicated to the city's other newspaper, the *Waterville Sentinel*; *De Molay Commandery*, dedicated to the Knights Templar unit in Skowhegan; and *Waterville*, which had been premiered and dedicated the previous year. Jean Missud, in Salem, Massachusetts, published Hall's *Barcelona Bolero* for cornet, a difficult and demanding solo, also in 1892.

In spite of the busy summer band season, and the dance work garnered by the Band Orchestra, once winter came opportunities for musical employment slacked off tremendously. As the new year approached band activity practically ceased, though a New Year's Day concert and ball was given by the Waterville Military Band. This was also the time of a sudden major business depression that sharply reduced people's ability to spend on entertainment or contribute to causes such as band fund drives. Waterville was particularly hard hit. The popular dancing instructor Haley, for whom Hall had provided so much music, and who had played violin in the Band Orchestra, moved to Belfast, believing conditions to be more favorable there. Hall was also that winter to make the first of his several brief attempts to break with Waterville.

In early February 1893, an announcement ran in the *Mail*, indicating Hall's interest in leaving.

Waterville people will regret that there is a chance they may lose the musical talent and ability of R. B. Hall, who has made his home in this city for two or more years, but who now has under consideration an offer to go to Springfield, Mass. to take a place in an orchestra in that city. Mr. Hall, as leader of the Waterville Military Band has done some very thorough work, and that has made the organization one of the best of its kind in the state. Mr. Hall is a pleasant, kind, social gentleman as well as a fine musician, and will be very much missed, if he shall conclude to accept the Springfield offer.[16]

This item, like so many similar announcements about Hall, is offered tentatively. The warm character appreciation was in the way of a farewell, albeit temporary. Hall was not in the Waterville news at all for the next thirteen weeks. He was obviously gone from the city for the entire remainder of the winter.

Whether he was in Springfield the entire time is doubtful. A flurry of publication activity ensued that indicates he probably went to

American Cadet March, by R. B. Hall. Solo Cornet part.[17]

Brockton, Massachusetts, to see Mace Gay who had published several of his marches in the past. It is also likely that he also went to Philadelphia to see Harry Coleman, who later published several of his marches and all of his schottisches, and who engraved and published first editions of many of the Hall marches that were later published by Carl Fischer.

Later that same year (1893) Hall's *American Cadet March*, dedicated to the American Cadet Band of Portland, Maine, was published by Carl Fischer. This march's

The High School Cadets March, by John Philip Sousa. Solo Cornet part.[18]

similarity in style and phrasing to Sousa's *The High School Cadets* caused controversy at the time and has often had bandsmen wondering if there were any copying in evidence. A close comparison of the two, reveals no direct copying of melody; but the phrase lengths, and formal schemes are identical. The charac-ter, both of the strains and the dynamics, alter-nates in the same way in both marches.

Some light may be shed on this question by examining an early edition. In addition to the dedicatory line, the Harry Coleman first-edition setting of Hall's *American Cadets*

March (also in 1893) carries above the title the surtitle: "Companion to the celebrated High School Cadets March." The key to their obvious similarity lies in the fact that these marches were used for the popular dances of the time. Dance masters in towns and cities throughout America, just like Bangor's Andrews, and Waterville's Dinsmore and Haley, with whom Hall worked, needed new music for each season's dance crazes. Just as dance fads today depend upon a certain char-acter in their music to cue the dancing, and generate similar pieces as long as the dance remains popular, at that time dancing was, if anything, more popular, and dance patterns more intricate. Hall's march was obviously designed to be used for the same dance steps and routine as the already popular Sousa march.

Harry Coleman had been the first copy-right holder for both Sousa's *High School Cadets* and Hall's *American Cadet March*. Carl Fischer published the pop-ular editions of both marches. Only a very few of Carl Fischer's editions of Hall's Marches bear the phrase "International Copyright." *American Cadet March* is not one of them. This may be more a result of the lack of space at the bottom of the page for an additional copyright notice than of any lack of diligence on the part of the publisher. The fact that Harry Coleman's editions were copy-righted in London, and Carl Fischer's were not, although an interesting observation, is not of major importance.

During the remainder of 1893 several more Hall titles were published by Mace Gay: *Dallas*, dedicated to the Dallastown, Pennsylvania, Odd Fellows lodge; *R.L.I.B.*, dedicated to the Richmond, Virginia, Light Infantry Blues Band; and *Appleton*, which bears no dedicatory inscription. Several possible ascriptions for this march will be discussed later.

With Hall gone, the Waterville musical scene adjusted to his absence by filling in with other local music. A dance at Taylor's dance hall, unable to get R. B. Hall, used Dinsmore as a solo fiddler, that is, without his orchestra at all. Dinsmore demonstrated that he still had skill, endurance, and appeal as a fiddler by keeping the crowd on their feet dancing "under the spell of the magic bow" for four hours.[19] In spite of the fact that Hall was away, the band fair, which had attained the status of an annual event to raise funds for the band, was held in early April. A minstrel show mounted by the band members was the main attraction, and "kept City Hall filled to overflowing" for three nights. The popular appeal of minstrel shows as entertainment was undisputed. As the *Mail* acknowledged: "a minstrel show always draws a good crowd in Waterville."[20]

Two pupils of R. B. Hall, Misses Fuller and Horne, were featured on the program, and at the grand concert and ball which closed the fair. Little else is known about Hattie Fuller, but Florence Louise Horne, who had moved to Waterville in 1892 at age twelve to study with Hall, later became a nationally-known touring soloist, and was billed as the leading lady cornetist of her day. At the 1893 Waterville Military Band Fair, she played *Rocked in the Cradle of the Deep* with variations, considered a very difficult piece for a young cornetist at that time. Written by Connecticut band master and cornetist Thomas H. Rollinson (1844-1928) this is an appealing solo that is used by cornetists and euphonium players even to this day, and never fails to please an audience. The *Mail* gave Miss Horne (age 13 at the time) a very favorable review.[21]

With full houses and enthusiastic publicity, the band cleared $500 from this year's (1893) three-days' venture, twice what had been raised the previous year. In spite of the generous profit additional funding would still be required if summer concerts were to be assured. Civic leaders from Skowhegan who attended the show were sufficiently impressed, and hired the Waterville Military Band to produce the same show for "fast day eve" (the Maine version of Mardi Gras.)[22]

Although no news of Hall had been printed in the *Mail* throughout February and March, by the end of April he had returned to Waterville and to the news. With Hall out of town and the business depression in its depths, no allocation had been made for summer concerts in Waterville that season. Soon it was announced that he would instruct the Bangor Band for the summer of 1893. At least partly because of his many students in Waterville, including the talented Misses Fuller and Horne, he chose to continue to reside there in spite of the lack of city funding for band concerts.

Prof. R. B. Hall has been engaged to instruct the Bangor Band, and went over for the first time, Wednesday. Prof. Hall will continue to have his headquarters in Waterville, however, and will lead the Waterville Military Band as heretofore.[23]

The Waterville Military Band continued with Hall as leader, in spite of the fact that he was gone a great deal to Bangor and elsewhere that summer. John Daily was named drum major, and attracted a fair bit of attention with his flamboyant style at parades. The band played at both the Waterville and Skowhegan parades on Memorial Day, and because of their several engagements in Waterville, where the largest Memorial Day celebration ever was being held, had a special train to run them to Skowhegan and back on their tight schedule.

The Germania Band of Boston played the Colby commencement that year, and received a lengthy and favorable review. Although Hall was later to become strongly associated with the annual Colby commencements, that time had not yet arrived for him. Directed by Emil Mollenhauer,[24] the Germania Band, a popular and well-established band from Boston, made quite a stir in Waterville with a lengthy and very classical program.

The Waterville Military Band was quite busy with excursions and fraternal outings, despite the lack of a season of park concerts. On Saturday June 24, 1893, they premiered a new march by Hall that he had written expressly for an outing of the Dunlap Commandery of Knights Templars.

The Waterville Military Band goes to Bath today to accompany the Dunlap Commandery K. T. of that city on a pilgrimage to Portsmouth, N.H. on Saturday. Prof. R. B. Hall, the leader of the band, has composed a special march for the occasion dedicated to the commandery, to be known as the "Dunlap Commandery March."[25]

Hall's *Dunlap Commandery March* was published in 1894 by Carl Fischer. It is a strong six-eight march, typical of Hall's best mature style, full of rich harmonizations, second beat accents and countermelodies. It has a six measure introduction, rather than the more usual four.

EXAMPLE 6. Dunlap Commandery March by R. B. Hall, measures 1-6 of the solo cornet part.[26]

The first part of the two-strain trio is characterized by unusual crescendos and surprising dynamic contrasts:

EXAMPLE 7. Dunlap Commandery March by R. B. Hall, Trio, measures 41-66 of the solo cornet part.[27]

Written to be played on this outing, *Dunlap Commandery* is scored so that the full effect can be had with a band of only about 24 players, which is what Hall knew he would have on that day. This is one of the reasons that Hall's marches have been such enduring favorites among smaller bands: they were written with a small band in mind.

Two other outings that summer were to inspire marches from Hall. The First Maine Regiment of the Uniformed Rank Knights of Pythias took an August excursion to their field day in Bath, where they met with the Sir Knights Belfast Division. A band concert at the Alameda Hotel ensued, and the following day the groups took an excursion aboard the steamer Kennebec to Fort Popham beach for a clambake. The site of the 1607 new colonial attempt at the mouth of the Kennebec by Sir George Popham (1550-1608), Fort Popham was developed into an impressive fortification during the War of 1812, and became an important tourist destination in Hall's era. It is now a state park.

Hall's march *Fort Popham* was published in 1895 by Carl Fischer. Since it was premiered by the Waterville Military Band on January 1, 1894, it was not available for this excursion, but was more than likely titled in hopes of repeating the engagement the following season. *Fort Popham* is an alla-breve (cut-time) march that, although not as elaborate as *Dunlap Commandery*, has several musically interesting features. It starts with a half-measure pickup (up-beat) and the introduction is strongly syncopated.

EXAMPLE 8. Fort Popham March by R. B. Hall, measures 1-9 of the solo cornet part.[28]

The melody is in the bass instruments for the first and second strains, with the higher voices playing a rhythmic countermelody. A quiet melodic trio finishes the march. Harmonized in thirds and featuring a dip to the lower neighbor and return (a characteristic Hall melodic gesture) it is the type of trio melody that is found on so many of Hall's better-known marches that it came to be regarded by bandsmen as "a typical Hall trio."

EXAMPLE 9. Fort Popham March by R. B. Hall, Trio, measures 48-80 of the solo cornet part.[29]

Through much of the summer of 1893 Hall was reported as being away from Waterville. A typical news item is the following:

R. B. Hall, the leader of the Waterville Military Band and Maine's most talented cornet player, is playing concerts in the Eastern part of the State with a number of Bangor musicians.[30]

This news reflects the fact that Hall was also the director of the Bangor Band that season. Although that was not of concern to his Waterville public, his absence was noted, especially in a season when the usual outdoor concerts were not being given by the Waterville Military Band.

In spite of being away a great deal, Hall managed visits to his home town of Richmond, Maine, and many excursions with the Waterville Military Band including a "Grand" concert at Maranacook that included spiritualists as speakers. It was advertised widely and excursion trains ran to Maranacook from all parts of the state.

In addition to *Fort Popham*, inspired by the Knights of Pythias field day, a field day held by the Second Regiment Patriarchs Militant in Bangor was to inspire a march for that group. An elaborate conclave held the third weekend in September, it involved

EXAMPLE 10. *March Second Regiment Patriarchs Militant by R. B. Hall. Solo Cornet part.[33]*

Patriarchs lodges from all over Maine, and a regiment from Massachusetts as well.

Canton Halifax will assemble and be escorted by the Waterville Military Band, R. B. Hall, leader. The arrival in Bangor will be about noon and the chevaliers will

be quartered at the different hotels in the city, Canton Halifax going to the Windsor.[31]

The grand street parade was to involve 400 to 500 "chevaliers." Several bands were referred to as "chevaliers," and sometimes "cavaliers," in connection with their lodge activities. This usage occasionally spilled over to the Knights of Pythias members, as well.) On Sunday, after a band concert at Norumbega Hall, a boat trip down the Penobscot River to Islesboro with a clambake at Rider's cove was planned. The return to Bangor would be "in time for the cantons to catch the evening trains for home."[32]

The following winter, Hall introduced a new march, titled for, and perhaps inspired by the Second Regiment Patriarchs Militant field day.

Second Reg't P. M. was premiered by the Waterville Military Band on January 1, 1894, and published in 1894 by Carl Fischer. The printed parts bear a formal dedication to the Patriarchs Militant. A big-sounding six-eight march, it is filled with rich harmonies, second beat accents, and countermelodies. An especially bold second strain contains trumpet fanfares and a pistol shot, but is nicely balanced by a quiet, melodic trio.

An idea that later was to become an important musical phenomenon for Maine began September, 1893: choral conductor and organizer Carl Zerrahn[34] came to Waterville to organize the first "Statewide Grand Music Festival,"[35] a gathering of local choruses from small towns all over the state. The choral groups rehearsed individually in their home areas, and then gathered in Waterville for a week of rehearsing and performing. The new festival caught the musical public by storm, and for a month little else of musical interest could claim the public's attention.[36] After the festival was completed in mid-October and declared a fantastic success, Zerrahn Clubs sprang up all over the state to sing good music and prepare for the following year. R. B. Hall was chosen to lead the Waterville Zerrahn Club, with President Whitman of Colby to be its president and organizer.[37] After the festival the newspapers were flooded with editorials and letters recommending the teaching of vocal music in every elementary school in the state and promoting community singing.[38] M. H. Andrews, from Bangor, attended the festival. His state-wide reputation and position of musical respect was such that his presence in Waterville for the event seemed to convey an imprimatur of local appropriateness.[39]

Although the Zerrahn festivals were only to last two years, the groundwork was laid for William Rogers Chapman's Maine Music Festivals. These were to become a regular feature of Maine's musical life for 30 years, from 1897 to 1926.[40]

Hall's position as leader of the Waterville Zerrahn Club was destined to be short lived. The local organizer of the festival had sustained financial losses in mounting the monumental extravaganza, and with the help of the Zerrahn Club attempted to produce a benefit concert to make up the deficit. Unfortunately the October benefit concert was a financial disaster, and only netted $25.[41]

As the fall progressed, Hall and the hundred-plus Zerrahn devotees planned to produce Handel's oratorio *Esther* in hopes of raising some of the difference, but the date kept getting pushed back. By the end of December the headlines read: "Will the club go for another quarter?"[42] Not prominent but definitely an issue, was the matter of recompense for Hall as conductor of the club's weekly rehearsals. By early January the club had been suspended indefinitely.

The Waterville Military Band's New Year's concert and ball was a well publicized event that year, and generated strong interest with a lengthy announcement. Neither New Year's 1882 nor 1883 had been publicized for the band, though this year's ball was called the "third annual." In those previous years, Dinsmore's Orchestra had gotten notices for their New Year's ball at Soper's hall, but the Waterville Military Band had been entirely left out of the news. For this, their third annual ball, there was no lack of publicity. Two new marches were to be premiered, and several of Hall's arrangements were also to be given for the first time. The entire program is shown in Figure 3, the poster for the event.

Because the announcement in the Mail shows just how far Hall and the band had come in three years it is worth reading in its entirety.

The third annual New Year's concert and ball by the Waterville Military Band will be given at city hall Monday evening January 1. A fine concert programme has been prepared with several new numbers arranged by Prof. Hall, which will be played for the first time by the band at this concert. Among the others there will be a march dedicated to the Second Maine Regiment Partiarch's Militant; another will be a sextette from Lucier[sic], arranged by Prof. Hall, and a concert mazurka also arranged by Prof. Hall. There are fourteen numbers on the order of dances to follow the concert. The Waterville band is fast coming into prominence as one of the finest in Maine. It has already been engaged by Dunlap Commandery K. T. of Bath for the annual pilgrimage in June, and several other orders are already booked for the summer of 1894. Whenever the band furnishes music for any occasion it is almost certain to secure a re-engagement.[43]

FIGURE 3. *New Year's concert poster, January 1, 1894. (Courtesy of Bagaduce Music Lending Library, Blue Hill, Maine)*

As this announcement makes clear, the band was looking ahead very optimistically to another good year for excursions and fraternal affairs. This notice also fixes the date for first performance of Hall's *Second Regiment P. M.* and makes clear that it was not composed for the September field day, but rather afterward.

The mention of the "sextette from Lucier" is of course a reference (with misspelling, possibly due to the central Maine accent) to the famous second act sextet "Chi mi frena in tal momento?" from Gaetano Donizetti's opera *Lucia di Lammermoor* which was enjoying phenomenal popularity in the United States since being given a fresh production at the Metropolitan Opera in 1883. Hall's arrangement has unfortunately not survived to the present. It was more than likely among the music that was burned in the furnace for heat after the Waterville Military Band's headquarters at 93 Main street was taken over by the American Legion.[44]

Numerous bandsmen have remarked on the apparent similarity between the melodies in Hall's *Marche Funebre* and those of the sextet from *Lucia*. A close inspection of the two, where they have been transposed to the same key for ease of comparison, shows that the first six measures of the trio of Hall's march are identical in harmonic movement and extremely similar in melodic contour to Donizetti's sextet. In the seventh measure the

EXAMPLE 11. R. B. Hall, Marche Funebre, measures 28-35, transposed to key of C. (Originally in A-flat)[45]

harmonies become different. In the eighth measure they diverge, as Donizetti's melody must extend to fill a longer form, but each comes back to restate the main melody and its restful harmony once more. A logical question to be asked is: was Hall's borrowing conscious, unconscious, or a deliberate quotation?

Marche Funebre was published in 1901 by Carl Fischer, but it is impossible to say when Hall actually made his manuscript of the march. Several other pieces that he had published in 1900 and 1901 had their first performances as much as five years earlier, and were even engraved by Harry Coleman years

in advance of their Fischer or John Church releases.

We will probably never really know if Hall penned the trio to *Marche Funebre* while his arrangement of the famous sextet was fresh in his mind. It is possible that he considered the line so famous that a deliberate quotation

EXAMPLE 12. G. Donizetti, "Chi mi frena in tal momento," from Lucia di Lammermoor, measures 2-10, transposed to key of C. (Originally in D-flat.)[46]

would be obvious, like the times he quoted "Annie Laurie." In any event it should take nothing away from the enjoyment of the march to know that this connection exists.

The Waterville Military Band's 1894 New Year's ball had a very good review, both concert and dancing. The *Mail* selected the Second Regiment P. M. as the evening's favorite; the reviewer waxed eloquent.

The first number, a march dedicated to the Second Maine Regiment Patriarchs Militant, composed by the leader of the band, R. B. Hall, is one of the best of the many good things Hall has written. There is a full swinging movement to it just suited to march by. This march is sure to meet with great favor. There isn't a dull place in it.[47]

After the huge success of the New year's ball and the first performances of so many of his new pieces, Hall's activities were at a peak. Health problems, however, as in so many years, were to dominate his winter and spring. Although he appeared as a soloist at a benefit social given in mid-January, by the end of the month he was seriously ill. At the beginning of February the *Mail* reported him as having been "ill for a week."[48] In the very same issue of the *Mail*, directly across the fold from the story on Hall that described him as sitting up "for the first time since he was taken sick," was an item interesting to scholars in search of sources for Hall's march titles. Sharing the page with a story on the summer resort business and predictions for the coming resort season (which you can be sure he looked at) was a huge full-column headline reading "VENI- VIDI-VICI."[49] The familiar quotation from Caesar[50] was used as an advertisement for Dr. Greene's Nervura, a patent medicine sure to cure all types of illnesses. "If you are suffering, use Nervura the conqueror of disease and your system will be freed of complaints."[51] One wonders if Hall tried Nervura in this nasty bout with illness that kept him in bed and away from his cornet throughout the winter months. The next time Hall was actually reported playing the cornet was in May.

Many different explanations have been offered for Hall's march title *Veni Vidi Vici,* which was published in 1896 by John Church. Among them are various versions of the idea that Hall "Came, Saw, and Conquered" the Waterville Military Band, the American Cadet Band, or the Tenth Regiment Band. The publication date of 1896 makes any of the three possible. But these explanations all fail to take into account Hall's characteristic modesty and self-effacing nature to which all the informants for his biography who actually knew him allude. It would have been uncharacteristic for him to have engaged in any such bragadoccio. It is just as unlikely that Hall selected the title just because the phrase was current and would be sure to get a look from potential march customers. Rather, it is more likely that Hall selected the popular phrase for another reason, and its connection with the popular patent medicine is possibly one. We will probably never know if Hall actually used the medicine and liked the slogan, but it remains an intriguing possibility.

During the spring months, while Hall was out of circulation with illness and recovery, the *Mail* kept his name before the public with occasional progress reports on his illness, and a tale of Waterville visitors to New York City who were astonished to hear Hall's music popularly played as a prelude to theatrical performances there. The spring band fair once again featured a minstrel show by the "W.M.B. Minstrels," and solos by Hattie Fuller and Louise Horne.[52] Once again a plea was made for funds to support the band.

Although Hall had been out of circulation all spring, by mid-May he was once again playing his cornet, and the *Mail* carried news of his engagements in Bangor, Bar Harbor, and locally. Chandler's Band, however had managed to secure the Colby commencement concert.

If there was ever a penalty for being too consistently good, Hall paid it when the editors ran out of words of praise for his moving performances and the enthusiastic applause they engendered. A lengthy review of a concert in Waterville's city hall included the remark that "Prof. R. B. Hall gave his cornet solos with the same effect that usually marks his efforts."[53]

The parks in Waterville had been newly named by the city council that spring, and every effort was made to call attention to events in Monument Park, where the band usually gave its weekly open air concerts, The editors of the *Mail* pointed out that this was a privilege enjoyed by citizens of Waterville to listen to such a fine band at weekly concerts. "The band is now one of the very finest in the State, and has been drilling for many months on first class concert work."[54] Following the end of the business depression, the city could now afford to indulge in park improvements as well as a summer concert series. New electric lights for the band stand and settees for the audience would be provided that year.[55]

Less excursion business was reported during the summer of 1894, although the band did go to Bangor for the Fourth of July, and played the Dunlap Commandery pilgrimage to Boston, where they were favorably reviewed in the Boston Herald. A political campaign afforded some work for the band, with lots of work for the Republicans, who held rallies and electric street car parades, with the band as a featured part of the festivities.

The *Mail*'s interest in the band scene is an indication of how important the band was to the people of Waterville at the time. Band news was of interest, and although during this period the paper did not announce regular rehearsals or concerts, it did notice any unusual activities of the band. Few band engagements were reported in the *Waterville Mail* through September of 1894 into the fall and winter, reflecting the usual pattern in which orchestra work predominated in the cold months while the band hibernated.

Appearances by Hall's Orchestra were reported throughout October, November, and December, with only one appearance by the Waterville Military Band on November 20. A lengthy review of an evening of entertainment presented on Tuesday, December 4, which included Hall's Orchestra, stated that: "The cornet solo by Mr. Hall was especially fine, and was given in his best style."[56] Hall's orchestra was busy in December, and ushered in the new year with a concert and ball at City Hall. On January 11, the *Mail* reported an appearance by Hall in St. John, New Brunswick given the previous Monday, and quoted extensively from the glowing review printed in the Saint John *Globe.*

A few days later, in what was probably his last appearance before leaving for Albany, Hall "rendered fine cornet solos" at a banquet and dance held by the Dunlap Commandery, F. and A. M., at China, Maine on Tuesday evening, January 15. Hall's Orchestra played until the "small hours."[57] Hall departed at the end of January, 1895, for a new position with the Tenth Regiment Band in Albany, New York.

NOTES

1 *Waterville* [Maine] *Mail*, 11 March 1892, 2. (Hereafter *WM*).

2 Ibid.

3 Ibid., 3.

4 *WM*, 18 March 1892, 2.

5 Ibid.

6 Written by Foster in 1851 for E. P. Christy (leader of Christy's Minstrels) to sing, *Old Folks at Home* was published under Christy's name, and Christy kept the copyright. In spite of that, the song was later strongly identified with Foster, and was his biggest hit, although he never recieved any income from it. H. Wiley Hitchcock, *Music in the United States: A Historical Introduction*, (Englewood Cliffs, New Jersey: Prentice- Hall, 1969), 109, 112. John Tasker Howard, *A Treasury of Stephen Foster*, historical notes, (New York: Random House, 1946), 10, 87.

7 *WM*, 18 March 1892, 2.

8 Ibid.

9 Meacham's name was given with the title *American Patrol* in all announcements and reviews, to differentiate it from Norvello's *American Patrol*, which had wide exposure with Gilmore's touring band for ten years before Meacham introduced his piece of the same name and character. Composer Frank W. Meacham (1856?-1909) wrote his *American Patrol* for piano in 1885. It was first published for band in 1891 by Carl Fischer. Meacham's piece is remembered and played today; Norvello's has been long forgotten.

10 R. B. Hall, March *Canton Halifax*, (Brockton, Massachusetts: Mace Gay, 1892).

11 *WM*, 5 February 1892.

12 *WM*, 4 March 1892.

13 *WM*, 18 March 1892.

14 *WM*, 3 April 1892, 3.

15 This was to be Patrick Gilmore's last tour in Maine: he died September 23, 1892. The Gilmore Band under Victor Herbert would appear in Skowhegan the following year, but only a handful of Gilmore's men were involved, the rest having gone over to Sousa's new band.

16 *WM*, 3 February 1893, 3.

17 R. B. Hall, *American Cadet March*, (Philadelphia, Pennsylvania: Harry Coleman, 1893).

18 John Philip Sousa, *The High School Cadets*, (New York: Carl Fischer, 1890).

19 *WM*, 31 March 1893.

20 *WM*, 14 April 1893.

21 *WM*, Ibid.

22 Ibid.

23 *WM*, 28 April 1893, 3.

24 Emil Mollenhauer (1855-1927), a violinist, pianist, transcriber and arranger, led the Germania Band of Boston from 1889 to 1897, and the Boston Municipal band from 1897 to 1903, after which it became the Boston Band. Rehrig, *Heritage Encyclopedia of Band Music*, 532.

25 *WM*, 23 June 1894, 3.

26 R. B. Hall, *Dunlap Commandery March*, (New York: Carl Fischer, 1894), m. 1-6.

27 Ibid., m.41-66.

28 R. B. Hall, *Fort Popham March*, (New York: Carl Fischer, 1895), m. 1-9.

29 Ibid., m. 48-80.

30 *WM,* 14 July 1893, 3.

31 *WM*, 8 September 1893, 2.

32 Ibid.

33 R. B. Hall, *2nd Reg't P.M.*, (New York: Carl Fischer, 1894).

34 Carl Zerrahn (Karl Zerrahn, b. 1826 Malchow, Germany; d. 1909 Milton, Massachusetts) was a music educator and conductor. Conductor of the Germania Orchestra and the Handel and Haydn Society in Boston, he became a disciple of Lowell Mason, and wrote the important first educational music books for publisher Oliver Ditson. With Ditson's support he organized clinics, festivals, and summer workshops in many states to promote music teaching in the schools.

35 *WM*, 22 September 1893.

[36] *WM*, 6 October 1893.

[37] *WM*, 13 October 1893.

[38] Ibid.

[39] *WM*, 6 October 1893.

[40] Conductor and composer William Rogers Chapman, (b. 1855 Hanover, Massachusetts; d. 1935 Palm Beach, Florida) of New York City and Bethel, Maine. Best known for the Maine Festivals, he was also conductor of the New York Apollo Club and, for a time, the New York Philharmonic Society. Charles Eugene Claghorn, *Biographical Dictionary of American Music*, (West Nyack, N.Y.: Parker Publishing Co., 1973), 90. Edwards, *Music and Musicians of Maine*, 221-223, 378.

[41] *WM*, 27 October 1893.

[42] *WM*, 29 December 1893, 3.

[43] Ibid.

[44] NA#2228.055.

[45] R. B. Hall, *Marche Funebre*, (New York: Carl Fischer, 1901) Reduced from the band arrangement and transposed by Gordon W. Bowie.

[46] Gaetano Donizetti, "Chi mi frena in tal momento," *Lucia di Lammermoor*, (New York: G. Schirmer, Inc., 1898), 109-110. Condensed, extracted, and transposed by Gordon W. Bowie.

[47] *WM*, 5 January 1894, 3.

[48] *WM*, 2 February 1894, 3.

[49] Ibid.

[50] Actually Plutarch; we can't be really sure Caesar actually said or wrote this phrase, only that Plutarch ascribed it to him.

[51] Ibid.

[52] *WM*, 27 April 1894.

[53] *WM*, 25 May 1894, 3.

[54] *WM*, 8 June 1894, 3.

[55] Ibid.

[56] *WM*, 7 December 1894.

[57] *WM*, 18 January 1895.

[58] R.B. Hall, *March Creole Queen*. (Cincinnati, Ohio: The John Church Co, 1900)

CHAPTER SIX
HALL'S VISIT TO ALBANY, NEW YORK (1895)

Much attention has been given to Hall's work with the Tenth Regiment Band of Albany, New York. To a generation of bandsmen this period had seemed the epitome of his career. The band itself was well-known and well-liked, Albany was more populous and active than Waterville, and three of Hall's best known marches had titles pertaining to his Albany connections. Hall's march Tenth Regiment (published in 1895 by Carl Fischer) was his biggest hit up to that time.

In spite of this perception, Hall's stay in Albany was really rather brief. His association with Albany was during the first six months of 1895, when he took over the Tenth Regiment Band for a continuous period from late January to late May, acting as leader and manager. Hall left Albany to return to Maine at the end of May, before the busy summer season began in earnest. Newspaper accounts place Hall still in Waterville, Maine, on January 14, 1895 with a review of his cornet solos at the Masonic hall in China, Maine (located just east of Waterville)[1] and again on May 21, when, after a parade with the band, he was being welcomed back after his absence.[2]

Hall's Albany association yielded three marches: *Tenth Regiment*, *Albanian*, and *Col. Fitch,* all copyrighted by Carl Fischer in 1895. Each of these titles has an obvious connection with Hall's activities there.

Hall's brief sojourn in Albany reflects a struggle for leadership in the band scene there, which was intensified by the addition of an outside personality into an already competitive situation. Before Hall's arrival, Albany's Tenth Regiment Band and Orchestra was established under the leadership of John Gartland, and the Albany City Band and Orchestra was led by Augustus Elgie, with G. Freberthuyser as manager. In addition several other ensembles advertised for engagements in the city directory and newspapers, including the Albany Cadet Band; the Capitol Banjo, Mandolin, and Guitar Orchestra; the Cyprus Band; Gargusi's Orchestra; and Padula's Orchestra.

The Tenth Regiment Band itself was not at that time actually a part of the New York National Guard, due to an odd quirk of military history. According to the muster rolls and adjutant-general's reports, the Tenth Regiment was disbanded in 1881, and reorganized as the Tenth Battalion. At that time the band was dropped from the table of organization. There were four companies, a field staff, and a hospital corps; in some years a drum major was listed (but not 1894, 1895 or 1896); but there was no band until 1900, when a field music of 16 men and a first sergeant were enlisted or joined by transfer. After that time there was a regular entry for the band at every muster.

It should be noted, however, that during the days before the First World War enlistment records were not as strictly kept as they are now, especially where musicians were concerned. Often a signature was all that was required to participate in National Guard camp; sometimes the records were not even preserved. Musicians would "muster in" just for the duration of an encampment or a drill, then "muster out" to collect the musicians' pay, which was more than that of regular soldiers. The value of band music to military camp life was such that this situation was tolerated, particularly in years when the unit did not support a regular band.

During the 1890's the Tenth Regiment Band was not actually a part of the national guard, but rather a civilian organization. It filled the duties of a military band for the Tenth Battalion, and capitalized in its pursuit of civilian engagements on popular nostalgia for the more prosperous days of the Tenth Regiment before it had been reduced in size and funding to a battalion.

Nevertheless, the affairs of the band were very much a part of the history of the Tenth, whether as a Regiment or a Battalion. Even during the middle 1890's when the band was not mustered in, it still was engaged to play parades and balls for the Battalion, to go to camp, and to march and play at all the drills.

William E. Fitch was named Lieutenant Colonel in 1883 and took command of the newly reorganized and downsized Tenth Battalion.[3] He named John Gartland band leader that same year. In spite of the fact that we know R. B. Hall to have led the band during 1895, the history of the band does not reflect this: no other changes are noted in the military leadership of the band until Col. Fitch retired in 1897. He was succeeded by Major Stackpole who, as one of his first acts, named Augustus Elgie as band leader.[4] It is possible that Hall is not mentioned in the Band's history because he never enlisted in the Albany National Guard,

and also because his stay in Albany was so brief.

Traced through articles and advertisements in the Albany *Evening Journal* (Albany's leading general newspaper at the time) Hall's association with the Tenth Regiment Band began in January of 1895. John Gartland, who had been listed as director of the Tenth Regiment Band in its City Directory advertising since 1890, began on January 5th, 1895, to run an advertisement in the Entertainment section of the Albany *Evening Journal* to the effect that "Gartland's Band and Orchestra has no affiliation with any other Band." An article in the January 29, 1895, Albany *Evening Journal* states that R. B. Hall was elected "leader and director of the Tenth Regiment Band and Orchestra."[5] On February 5th, R. B. Hall's advertisement for the Tenth Regiment Band And Orchestra appeared in the amusements section. Thus began a pattern which was to persist throughout the winter and spring months. On Tuesday, Hall's advertisement; on Wednesday, Gartland's Band and Orchestra; on Thursday, Hall's; and on Saturday, both advertisements ran.

City directory advertising for Hall's band from that spring emphasized reliability, a modern sound and the best performers.

R. B. Hall's advertisement from the Albany City Directory, 1895.[6]

Gartland's advertisement in the same directory showed that his band had adopted the name Gartland's Military Band, and indicated Gartland's long standing in the community.

It is interesting to note that both bands were headquartered in the same building, with Gartland advertising his office on the second floor.

Gartland's advertisement from the Albany City Directory, 1895.[7]

No change in the pattern of newspaper advertising occurred until on Saturday, April 27, a Testimonial Concert for John L. Gartland was advertised for April 29, 1895. Gartland's Band was headed for Massachusetts, and for a tour including "work in Boston" for which they would be acclaimed even years later.[8]

Meanwhile, Hall had been ill, and returned, at least briefly, to Waterville to recuperate. This was noted in the Waterville press, but not in Albany where his absence seemingly went unnoticed. The *Waterville Mail* of March 22 noted that Hall had returned "suffering from a bilious attack."[9] The story continued to say that he found "his work in Albany pretty hard" because of the "good deal of marching to be done by the band."[10] Two weeks later he was well enough recuperated to be ready to resume his duties.

According to the *Mail*:

Prof. R. B. Hall leaves on the Pullman tonight to return to Albany, N.Y., where he will again take charge of the Tenth Regiment Band of that city. The local band made him a very good offer to remain here during the summer, but he is under obligation to the Albany organization and will continue there if his health is good enough for him to stand the hard work involved.[11]

Hall's health, which had always been fragile, was evidently taxed by his duties with the Tenth Regiment Band, especially the marching, which was made more difficult for him by his lameness. Hall carried a cane when marching, and stories from his youth had centered on this disability which never completely left him, even though this was less frequently mentioned as time went on. Although the Albany papers never mention it, Hall cited the large amount of marching as his reason for leaving when he decided to return to Waterville in May.[12]

The beginning of May was a busy time for Hall, and for the local music scene in Albany. Sousa's band had appeared at Bleecker Hall, on March 20, 1895, and offered a concert including works by Suppé, Wagner, Massanet, Chopin, and others; and including a new humoresque and a new march, *The Directorate*, by Sousa. Bleecker Hall was an upscale venue, with printed programs, and a regular schedule of visiting musical and theatrical events. Although Gilmore's and Sousa's bands had been regular annual attractions, the local bands never played there. But the soon-to-be newly organized Albania Orchestra would.

The *Evening Journal* for Monday, May 6, carried a story in the music news section announcing that R. B. Hall would be appearing as solo cornet with the Albania Orchestra under the baton of Mr. William J. Holding.[13] This was to be the beginning of the Albania Orchestra, a first for the city. By the next day a concert date had been set, and the "First Annual Concert of Albany Orchestra" was announced for May 15.[14]

As the week progressed, Gartland's regular advertisement appeared on Wednesday for the last time that spring, and Hall's regular advertisement on Thursday touted the Tenth Regiment Band and Orchestra. On Saturday, May 11, Gartland's band was not advertised. Hall's regular Saturday ad appeared as usual, and there was a new advertisement for the Albany Orchestra. Gartland was by then on tour, and so he had no need to advertise locally. On Tuesday, May 14, Hall's regular ad was included, and on Wednesday a large classified advertisement for the Albanian Orchestra touted its "first annual concert" to be given that night.[15]

Within the one short week that it had existed the Orchestra had used the names "Albania," "Albany," and "Albanian" interchangeably. This was in keeping with common usage at the time, however, which included advertising various firms as being "owned and managed by Albanians," and referring to the greater Albany area as "all Albania" in headlines, news stories, and advertisements.

The next day a front page review praised the orchestra. Hall was listed as first cornet, but not billed as a soloist, nor was a cornet solo given. The only march played was Sousa's *The Directorate*, which had been played there by Sousa's band two weeks previously. It had been featured as "new" on Sousa's programme, and was enjoying a flush of popularity. No R. B. Hall marches were performed at the Albania Orchestra concert.

On the following Saturday, May 18, a piece in the music news column (which seldom mentioned anything to do with band affairs) announced that Gartland's Band was to play the season in Saratoga at Congress Spring Park after finishing their engagement in Pittsfield, Massachusetts.[16] Col. William E. Fitch was designated parade marshal for the Memorial Day Parade.[17]

The very next day, an item announced that the Burgess Corps of the Albany National Guard was to be headed by Gartland's Band in the Memorial Day parade.[18] In all of these busy preparations for the city-wide celebration of an important patriotic occasion, the Tenth Regiment Band was not mentioned at all. Although no news in Albany marked the fact, R. B. Hall was already back in Waterville, Maine.[19] The Tenth Regiment Band was temporarily without a leader, although Augustus Elgie, who directed the City Band would soon take over that position.

On June 1, 1895, the Saturday paper carried a story announcing that Gartland's Band was chosen to play for Albany's Fourth of July celebration.[20] A separate item also announced the Tenth Regiment Band to give the first concert in the park for the summer season under the baton of Augustus Elgie.[21] That day, and for one more week, R. B. Hall's regular Tenth Regiment advertisement ran in the amusement section, in spite of the fact that Hall was already playing engagements in Waterville, and had indeed led the Waterville Military Band in the Memorial Day parade in that city.[22] On Tuesday, June 11, a new advertisement for the Tenth Regiment Band, with Augustus Elgie as leader, made its first appearance. Thereafter Hall's name was seen no more. The following week a story ran on Gartland's Band, describing them as "busier than ever."[23]

What accounted for Hall's speedy departure? Was he already engaged in Maine for the summer, before taking the Albany job? Or did he lose out in a fiercely competitive and saturated market, where he had attempted to displace a long time local favorite? Hall and Gartland had offices in the same building, on different floors. Gartland had a telephone, Hall did not. Hall advertised three times a week, Gartland only twice. Hall performed as a cornetist, apart from his band, Gartland did not. Hall was a composer of considerable reputation, Gartland was not. Gartland took his band on tour in Massachusetts, while Hall kept his in the Albany area. Gartland garnered more than twice the press that Hall did. Nothing in Albany gives the faintest clue as to the real answer to this question, but the *Waterville Mail*'s story on Hall's return makes it clear that he attributed it to his health, and the large amount of marching required of the Tenth Regiment Band. The date of the Waterville story, May 17, 1895, establishes that Hall had already made his decision to return to Maine at the time he played the Albania Orchestra concert.[24]

THE ALBANY BAND SCENE AFTER HALL

After Hall left Albany, the band competition continued at a feverish pace for several more years. Whereas in 1894 there were only four bands and orchestras to vie for the Albany public's attention, in 1895 there were eight, including Elgie, Hall and Gartland. In 1896 the City Directory listed eight bands (without Hall) including the Tenth Regiment Military Band and Orchestra with Augustus Elgie, Director. The band had moved its office to 75 State Street. Gartland's Military Band had combined with Gioscia's Orchestra, and they were still at 496 Broadway. Elgie's Albany City Band was no longer listed.

No directory is available for 1897, but by 1898 the names of the bands had shifted. Gartland's Tenth Regiment Band (and Gioscia's and Gartland's Orchestra) now occupied the office at 75 State, while Elgie's Tenth Battalion Band had moved down the block to 78 State. The change of names is in keeping with the military fact that Major Stackpole had named Elgie to leadership of the Battalion's band in 1897. By 1899 there were only four bands, including the new Empire State Band. The 1900 directory includes Gartland's Military Band and Elgie's Tenth Battalion Band. The year 1900 is also when the muster rolls of the Tenth Battalion begin once again to show an enlisted band at every muster, even though the band was down to eight or nine men for most of 1900 and 1901. Gioscia's Unrivaled Orchestra, which had been affiliated with Gartland's Band for the previous three years, was once again on its own.

In the 1901 City Directory, Gartland had reclaimed the Tenth Regiment name and the 75 State Street office, while Elgie still led the Tenth Battalion Band, but had moved the office again. Was this when Hall came back, however briefly, if indeed he actually did, to take the Tenth Regiment band to the Pan American Exposition? Subsequent years saw a continual decline in the number of bands advertised, size of the printing type used in their advertisements, stridency of claims in

their ads, and by 1905, no bands at all are advertised or listed in the City Directory.

THE SUMMER OF 1901: ALBANY BANDS AND THE PAN AMERICAN.

Of all of the phases of Hall's career, the one that has seemed most to fascinate previous writers is his time in Albany, where he was said to have "rebuilt the musically bankrupt band of the Tenth Regiment Albany National Guard on short notice."[25] The problem with this remark, however, is that it refers to a visit that Bardwell believed that Hall made to Albany for eleven months during 1900 and 1901; and to a trip to the Pan American Exposition in Buffalo, where Hall is said to have appeared with the Tenth Regiment Band for an engagement from the 26th to 31st of August, 1901.[26] Elsewhere, Bardwell attributes to Hall "more than a year" as conductor of the Tenth Regiment Band in Albany.[27]

There are two major problems with including an eleven- month Albany sojourn, culminating at the end of August, 1901, in the chronology of Hall's career. First, other records indicate that Hall was in residence in Waterville during that time. Second, there is no corroborating evidence in either Albany or Buffalo that places Hall there in 1900-01.

The summer of 1901 was a remarkable one for the bands in Albany. According to newspaper accounts Elgie's Tenth Battalion Band returned from its "tour of duty at the state camp" at Peekskill on Saturday, June 5.[28] They returned to a summer of controversy. The *Knickerbocker* of June 19 reports that the Independence Day Celebration committee had decided not to hold a parade.[29] There would, however, be band music after the morning orations on July 4, and a band concert in the park on July 6, the following Saturday, which had been declared a half-holiday.

On Friday, June 28, the Knickerbocker reported a controversy over the July 4 music and July 6 concert. The city comptroller had put the music out to bid, and a non-union band had underbid the established bands.[30] By July third, it was known whose band that was. The Albany *Evening Journal* reported that "Henzel's Band would furnish the music" for the morning orations.[31] Philip Henzel was president of the half-holiday association which was organizing the festivities for Saturday, July 6. Henzel, however, was not known as a bandleader. He did not advertise, and his band was not a regular part of the competitive band scene in Albany. Just what group of musicians is meant by "Henzel's Band" is questionable.

No other band music was mentioned in the *Evening Journal*, but the *Express-Knickerbocker* for July 3 ran a small item announcing that "Elgie's Tenth Regiment Band" would be appearing at Electric Park on the Fourth of July.[32] Electric park was a private amusement park owned by the Albany Hudson Railway Company. Vaudeville and band concerts were featured nightly, and admission was free to those who purchased a tram ticket to get there. According to regular advertisements in the Albany papers the Tenth Regiment Band under Elgie appeared there regularly throughout the entire summer season.

Lagoon Island, a pleasure park similarly owned by the steam ferry line, featured an all-female band for the entire summer, and made as much of their "angelic and maidenly" appearance as of the "sweet strains" of their music.[33]

The following week the papers were full of the controversy between city officials and the union musicians. The city had been required by its charter put the music for the Fourth of July out to bid, and Henzel's band was low bidder. A rebid later the same week produced the same results. The city had to reject bids from its three most prominent band leaders: Elgie, Gartland and Collins, all union men. When the comptroller refused to pay a non-union band, the Mayor and city attorneys had to order him to do so. The *Knickerbocker Express* for July 5th quoted the comptroller as saying the mayor "would lose the votes of all competent musicians in Albany."[34] On July 8, the unions denounced the mayor, although Elgie admitted that the mayor had "no choice under the charter."[35] The eventual union resolution was made in carefully guarded language, so as not to interfere with the public park concerts planned by the City and yet to be played by Collins and Gartland.

Saturday, July 6, was the official half-holiday, and a band concert was indeed given in Washington Park. Instead of the non-union band that had caused such a furor on the Fourth, this time Collins's Albany City Band, a union group, was used. The concert venue had been moved by the city for fear that the crowd would trample the newly planted shrubbery. Permission for fireworks and illuminations was denied on the same basis.[36]

Later that summer, when Company B of the Tenth Battalion announced its plans to go to Buffalo for its summer muster the week of August 3rd through 10th, 1901, they also announced, and the paper noted "there will be no band of music."[37] The bands were all too busy with their profitable summer employment to take time for military duty.

John Gartland's Tenth Battalion Band was playing every afternoon at Congress Spring Park in Saratoga. Augustus Elgie's Tenth Regiment Band was appearing nightly at Electric Park. Additionally, both leaders gave a series of evening concerts in the Albany public parks, usually Washington Park. Gartland every Tuesday, and Elgie on certain Saturday nights. Collins and the Albany City Band gave a concert every Thursday night. When a new park was proposed for the city, the main selling point for the public was that "band concerts are to be given weekly or oftener."[38]

Amidst all this band activity, there is not a word of mention about R. B. Hall. If he were in the city, and engaged in the business of band music, he could not have been so conspicuously absent from this active and well reported band scene. In 1895, when Hall was in Albany for only six months, his advertisements were seen several times a week, as well as occasional news of his concerts. In Waterville, Maine, that summer the papers carried frequent news of his appearances,[39] yet in Albany, in 1901, he is totally absent.

If the Tenth Regiment Band had gone to Buffalo, it could not have been kept secret from the press. Throughout the entire summer season, stories appeared regularly on just who was gone from Albany to Buffalo, to visit or appear at the Pan American Exposition. The *Knickerbocker* frequently asserted that any group which could, would find any excuse to make the trip. The attraction of the Pan American was so strong that transportation was in short supply, and service staff for Albany's hotels was hard to find that summer. Yet no mention of a band from Albany taking the trip is made in either paper, and in the week of August 26-31, during which Hall and the Tenth Regiment Band are said to have made the trip, there is no news of such a move by either the Tenth Battalion Band or the Tenth Regiment Band, both of which were pursuing their busy schedules in the Albany environs.

Meanwhile, back in Waterville, the *Waterville Mail* for April 17, had run a piece about Hall's financial arrangements with the Waterville Military Band for the summer series. On May 29, the paper advertised that R. B. Hall and the Waterville Military Band would lead the Memorial Day Parade, and present a concert in the afternoon. No interruptions to the regular summer concerts were noted by the *Mail*, and although they did not specifically mention Hall during the week of August 26 to 31, their pattern of announcing whenever he left town to perform elsewhere, or whenever a summer concert would be postponed or canceled due to Hall's absence, implies that Hall did not do anything unusual that week.

One band from Albany was indeed scheduled to play at the Pan American Exposition that summer. It was, however, not a well-known band in Albany. Robertson's Band was a new entrant in the commercial band field, led by cornet soloist Orville A. Robertson. The band's debut concert in January, 1901, was announced with a program and a glowing introductory story in the Albany *Evening Journal*.[40] A lukewarm review of the concert dispelled the high expectations that had been raised.[41] Robertson's Band received no further mention in the Albany press as the spring months ensued. The introductory concert had been held just at the time that plans for the Pan-American were being first announced to the public.[42]

Robertson's forty-piece band was described in the program pamphlet for the Pan American Exposition.[43] Interestingly, although all the other bands have a picture of the band included in the program, Robertson's Band shows only a portrait of Robertson and a few soloists in a montage; no group photo. Perhaps there was no group. In Albany, during the summer of 1901, Robertson played solo cornet for Collins' Albany City Band.[44] No stories, announcements or advertisements for Robertson's Band were to be found in the Albany papers. Possibly, Robertson had assumed that he could pick up enough musicians from Collins' and other Albany bands to make a forty-piece band just for the trip to Buffalo and had used the January 23 *Journal* announcement to help secure the engagement.

Could it be that Hall's Band replaced Robertson's Band at the Pan American on short notice? This view, too has been contended. Tom Bardwell's recollection of Jean Missud's personal diary, as he read it many years ago, suggests that Hall was indeed there, to replace Robertson's band, which "had an internal conflict" and did not appear.[45] According to Bardwell's recollection, Robertson had reneged on his contract as of July 21, 1901, and Hall was engaged to replace him with the 44-piece Tenth Regiment Band. Conveyed conversationally, this assertion is backed up with a reference to the program for the entire summer's music at the Pan American.[46] This rare pamphlet contains pictures and write-ups for all the bands, orchestras, organists, and soloists to appear at the Pan American that summer, and indicates that Jean Missud was indeed there, with his Salem Cadet Band from Salem, Massachusetts. A photocopy of Bardwell's copy of this program shows his marginal notes indicating the changes in the program that he recalled as having been noted by Missud. An unaltered copy obtained from the Library of Congress simply lists the bands as scheduled.

Although the program for the Pan American Exposition does indeed list Robertson's band for the dates in question, (August 26-31, 1901) a careful reading of the Buffalo newspapers for the entire summer reveals no mention of changes in the bands scheduled for that week.[47] The *Buffalo Evening News* reviewed two band concerts during the week of August 15. During the week in question it reviewed the premier of a march by The Mexican Artillery Band's leader, Capt. Pacheo, the *Emblem of Peace*.[48] On August 27 it mentioned Robertson's Band, and again on August 29 in two different articles mentioned Robertson's Band of Albany.[49] At the close of the week's activities the *Evening News* ran a piece about the changing bands, and a lengthy and detailed review of Capt. Thomas and the Havana Municipal Police Band in their farewell concert.[50] If Hall were performing there, it is inconceivable that the *Evening News* would have missed it. Did Hall possibly appear incognito, under Robertson's name? That does not appear likely, given what we know of Hall's career style.

Why, then, has the idea of Hall's appearing at the Pan American on these specific dates been so widely recirculated? It seems that in a biography so devoid of firm dates and hard facts, the assertion of those dates, however mistaken, was a quotable element that was never questioned or disputed, but simply recirculated, by writers such as Swift and Hudson, whose work followed Bardwell's. The matter of real and enduring importance is not, however, the issue of whether R. B. Hall appeared at the head of the Tenth Regiment Band in Buffalo in 1901, which I conclude he did not. The real issue is what happened to the Tenth Regiment Band after Hall's departure from the scene; did they carry Hall's tradition forward? Again my conclusion is that they did not. As the Tenth Regiment Band's record indicates, the R. B. Hall era in their history was only a few months, and they eventually were restored to active status in the battalion, and moved out of Albany altogether. Once they became headquartered in Queens County, New York, following World War I, the Tenth Regiment Band no longer had any Albany men. In the years prior to World War II they passed out of existence.

The legacy of Hall's time in Albany is vested entirely in his marches from that time, including *Albanian*, *Col. Fitch*, and *Tenth Regiment*. *Hamiltonian* has been postulated as belonging to this era in Hall's career, though there is a better explanation for its title in Waterville. So has *Veni Vidi Vici*, although here, again, events in Waterville offer a more likely context. The much later *Officer of the Day* has often been ascribed to Hall's association with the Tenth Regiment Band, but its composition probably does not have anything to do with his actual time in Albany.

NOTES

[1] *Waterville* [Maine] *Mail*, 18 January 1895. (Hereafter, *WM*).

[2] *WM*, 24 May 1895.

[3] *Annual Report of the Adjutant-General of the State of New York, for the Year 1896*, (Albany, New York: Wynkoop Hallenbeck Crawford Co., 1897), 64-65.

[4] Clarence S. Martin, *Seventy Five Years With the Tenth Regiment Infantry, N. Y. National Guard, 1860-1935*, (Albany, New York: J. B. Lyons Companies, 1935).

[5] *Albany* [New York] *Evening Journal*, 29 January 1895. (Hereafter *AEJ).

[6] *The Albany Directory for the Year 1895*, (Albany, New York: Sampson, Murdock & Co. Publishers, 1895), 813.

[7] Ibid., 781.

[8] *AEJ*, 5 January 1901, 2.

[9] *WM*, 22 March 1895.

[10] Ibid.

[11] *WM*, 5 April 1895.

[12] *WM*, 17 May 1895.

[13] *AEJ*, 6 May 1895, 7.

[14] *AEJ*, 7 May 1895.

[15] *AEJ*, 15 May 1895.

[16] *AEJ*, 18 May 1895.

[17] *AEJ*, 22 May 1895.

[18] *AEJ*, 23 May 1895.

[19] *WM*, 24 May 1895.

[20] *AEJ*, 1 June 1895.

[21] Ibid.

[22] *WM*, 24 May 1895, 7 June 1895.

[23] *AEJ*, 15 June 1895.

[24] *WM*, 17 May 1895. The story is quoted in its entirety in Chapter X in connection with Hall's return to the Waterville Military Band.

[25] Thomas C. Bardwell, Sr., "The New England March King," *Fanfare*, 1:10 (1977), 29.

[26] Ibid.

[27] Thomas C. Bardwell, Sr., "Robert Browne Hall (The New England March King)," *Music Journal Anthology 1968*, Ed. R. Cumming (New York, 1968), 33.

[28] *Daily Express Knickerbocker and Albany* [New York] *Morning Express*, 5 June 1901, 5. (The Saturday edition combined the morning and evening editions, hence the lengthy title). (Hereafter *KE*).

[29] *KE*, 19 June 1901.

[30] *KE*, 28 June 1901.

[31] *AEJ*, 3 July 1901.

[32] *KE*, 3 July 1901.

[33] *AEJ*, 23 July 1901, 8.

[34] *KE*, 5 July 1901, 2.

[35] *AEJ*, 8 July 1901, 1.

[36] *AEJ*, 6 July 1901, 10.

[37] *KE*, 11 July 1901, 2.

[38] *AEJ*, 29 July 1901, 8.

[39] *WM*, 29 May; 26 June; 7, 14, 21 August 1901.

[40] *AEJ*, 23 January 1901, 10.

[41] *AEJ*, 26 January 1901, 12.

[42] Ibid, 1.

[43] *Music at the Pan-American Exposition: Organists Orchestras Bands*, (Buffalo, N. Y.: n.p., 1901), 44.

[44] *AEJ*, 6 July 1901, 10.

NOTES, CONT.

[45] Jean M. Missud (1852-1941) was the founder and leader of the Salem Second Corps of Cadets Band from Salem, Massachusetts. A prolific composer himself, he was also a publisher, and published several of Hall's works.

[46] *Music at the Pan-American*, op. cit.

[47] *Buffalo* [New York] *Evening News*, (all editions) 14-31 August 1901. (Hereafter *BEN*).

[48] *BEN*, 26 August 1901.

[49] *BEN*, 27 August 1901, 29 August 1901.

[50] *BEN*, 31 August 1901.

CHAPTER SEVEN
RETURN FROM ALBANY TO WATERVILLE AND PORTLAND
(1895-1896)

While Hall had been in Albany during the winter of 1895, the Waterville Military Band had been dormant, although it did elect a new leader during that time. Its progress, and Hall's eventual return to Waterville, can be traced through announcements and editorials appearing in the *Waterville Mail* .

Although Hall was in Albany for the winter, he was not forgotten by the *Mail*, and when illness brought him back to Waterville for a brief recuperation, rumors began to circulate that he would eventually return to lead the Waterville Military Band. Thus on March 22 the *Mail* reported:

Prof. R. B. Hall has returned from Albany, suffering from a bilious attack, and the members of the Waterville Military Band are using their best endeavours to persuade him to remain here. Prof. Hall finds his work in Albany pretty hard, as there is a good deal of marching to be done by the band of which he is leader. There is a possibility that he may make up his mind to stay here.[1]

Hopes were dashed the following week, though, when the *Mail* announced that Hall would leave again. Health had always been a prominent issue in Hall's life, ever since his frail childhood. Here it emerges as the controlling factor in whether he would remain in Waterville, or leave again to resume his duties with the Tenth Regiment Band.

Prof. R. B. Hall leaves on the Pullman tonight to return to Albany N. Y. where he will again take charge of the Tenth Regiment Band of that city. The local band made him a very good offer to remain here during the summer but he is under obligation to the Albany organization and will continue there if his health is good enough for him to stand the hard work involved.[2]

The spring of 1895 brought a revival of band activity, first with rehearsals, then the regular concerts. With hope of Hall's return all but gone, the men in the band had to set about finding a new leader who could revitalize the band for the coming season.

The *Waterville Mail* first reported on February 15 that the Waterville Military Band had decided to hold a fair in April. The next news of this was on April 12 when the fair date was set for May 2 and 3. This April news was just one week after Hall refused to be persuaded to return, and his April departure for Albany had been reported. The surprise feature of the fair announcement was the introduction of the Band's new leader, Mr. Frank Knapp. The fair would feature cornet solos by the new leader. According to the *Mail* :

Mr. Knapp comes from Norway with excellent recommendations. He has been playing band music from early boyhood, and has had instruction from first class teachers.[3]

The *Mail* didn't clarify whether the new leader hailed from Norway, Maine, or Norway in Europe, but he evidently pleased the band as the following week's story pointed out.

Rehearsal of the Waterville Military Band under Mr. Knapp was held Tuesday evening. The members of the band were very much pleased by him and at the rehearsals to be held this evening the

arrangements for making him the leader of the band to succeed Mr. Hall will undoubtedly be completed. The band concerts last year were a great success and a few weeks later the city government will be asked to make an appropriation to help defray expenses as was done last year.[4]

Frank Knapp's term as leader of the Waterville Military Band was destined to be short. Although the band fair was held on schedule May 2 and 3, and received favorable reviews for its production of "Finnegan's Fortune" and the "Grand Band Concert" featuring Mr. Knapp's solos, only two weeks elapsed before the *Mail* announced his resignation together with the news that R. B. Hall had resigned in Albany.

According to the *Mail* :

Frank P. Knapp has resigned as leader of the Waterville Military Band and, fortunately for the band, the former leader, R. B. Hall signified his intention of giving up his position at Albany, N. Y., on account of the hard work involved in the large amount of marching done by the band of which he had been leader there. Mr. Hall will undoubtedly return to Waterville and will again take charge of the local organization. The members of the band are delighted to know that he is coming back.

The City Council has voted an appropriation for band concerts sufficient to help considerably in expenses of the band during the summer, and Waterville people will again have the privilege of listening to one of the best bands in the state, under the leadership of probably the best cornet player in New England.[5]

This article, in addition to announcing Knapp's resignation, gives Hall's reason for leaving Albany: too much marching. Stories from Hall's younger years frequently mention his lameness.[6] Later tales about Hall pointed out that he would march using his cane, holding the cornet with one hand. Whatever the cause of his lameness might have been, marching with a handicap is obviously difficult and tiring. As this article hinted, the Tenth Regiment Band in Albany demanded a great deal of marching, and so it stands to reason that Hall sought a situation where his lameness would be less of an issue.

Following his return from Albany in late May of 1895, Hall was to lead the Waterville Military Band through its summer season. By May 24, Hall was in Waterville, greeting friends who had missed him. Announcements for the Memorial Day parade touted the Waterville Military Band, R. B. Hall, leader, in the paradc position immediately behind the police and the letter carriers. Ironically, there may have been less marching, but nevertheless there was a parade Hall's very first week back in Waterville.

A week later Hall's Orchestra was engaged for the Waterville High School graduation. The first band concert of the season was given Tuesday, June 4, to a large and very appreciative crowd. That was unusually early to begin the summer series, which in most years didn't start until July. Enthusiasm for Hall's return was high.

The events of the summer of 1895 are worth examining in some detail because of the pattern in Hall's life to which they point. Hall was welcomed back to Waterville from Albany; the beginning of the summer season received a great deal of attention in the press. As the season progressed, however, the flurry of attention began to subside. There was not enough work to keep the band busy, and Hall's salary requirements were not being met by the band. Towards the summer's end rumblings could be heard that Hall would leave again, this time for Portland.

For the remainder of June, however, the paper described weekly concerts in glowing terms and published the program each week for the week to follow.[7] Usually the *Mail* merely announced the concert, but not the specific pieces to be played. By mid-July, however, the frenzy of press attention had calmed to the usual custom of announcing

only changes or missed concerts. Possibly the lack of press attention coincided with Hall's increasing interest in Portland.

A few other engagements of the band were reported in the paper as well. On July 5, it was reported that the Waterville Military Band had performed for the dedication of the Dexter Public Library in Dexter on July 3. The regular band concerts on Tuesday nights were in progress. Although Hall's name was not specifically mentioned in some of the concert notices, a postponement notice in August leads to the belief that Hall was present for the entire season, and after returning to leadership became once again indispensable to the band's appearances.

The Band concert was given Wednesday night instead of Tuesday night as usual, as Prof. Hall was engaged to go to Winthrop to take part in a recital given by Miss Maud Mayo of Auburn.[8]

This announcement is typical of the style of the *Mail* in these years. It was assumed that the concerts would go on as scheduled every Tuesday night, all summer long. The only newsworthy element was if the concert was canceled or postponed for some reason. This concert poster announces a sacred concert from about the same era. The program includes Missud's Magnolia Serenade, a solo

Concert Poster, July 17, no year given. (Courtesy Bagaduce Music Lending Library, Blue Hill, Maine)

that Hall performed frequently during these years.

The final piece of band news for the season came on September 13. In it the *Mail* reported that the Waterville Military Band had traveled to Shawmut (a small town about five miles north of Waterville) the previous Thursday to furnish music for a celebration and dedication of a new grammar school.

What is most noticeable about the announcements for the summer of 1895 is the comparative paucity of information concerning Professor Hall's activities. To be sure, the concerts by the Waterville Military Band were given as usual, but few other band engagements are noted. Dinsmore's Orchestra seems to have entirely faded from the scene. Hall's ultimate departure for Portland in the fall of that year may be both an explanation for and at least in part a result of the scarcity of band engagements that summer.

The *Waterville Mail* ran a long item on this matter that is worth quoting in its entirety.

R. B. Hall bade good bye to his friends in this city Monday before leaving for Portland where he has accepted an engagement as leader and director of the American Cadet Band. Mr. Hall has had charge of the Waterville Military Band for most of the last four years and has made it one of the best bands in the State. When he came here there were two band organizations in the city, but the members of the Lockwood band as it was known, soon cast in their fortunes with the musicians who were enjoying Mr. Hall's instruction. During his residence here Mr. Hall has written a number of band pieces, most of them marches, that are now played by bands all over the country. His sole reason for leaving Waterville lay in the fact that the field for band work here is not large enough to enable the organization to pay him a fair salary. Mr. Hall was most royally welcomed by the Portland band on his arrival in the city Monday evening. The whole band met him at Union Station and escorted him to the band rooms where a banquet was served in his honor. V. W. Libby, in behalf of the members, presented Mr. Hall with a handsome rosewood silver-mounted baton.[9]

This long and newsy account names Hall's dissatisfaction with his salary in Waterville as his reason for leaving. It also calls attention to Hall's success with the Waterville Military Band, and his popularity as a person as well as as a composer and band leader.

In October, Hall moved to Portland where he resided until May of 1896. The Portland city directory for 1896 lists R. B. Hall as a music teacher having home and office at 59 Hampshire Street. He also had a listing in the music teachers' section of the directory, but no mention was made of any leader in the listing for the American Cadet Band. By 1897, Hall was no longer listed in the Portland directory, but his sister Vinnie was, at the same address.

The American Cadet Band was a focus of Hall's activities while he was in Portland, as the following quote from Edwards' discussion of professional bands and orchestras in the State of Maine points out.

R. B. Hall, who, at that time, was enjoying exceeding popularity as a composer, then took the leadership of the band and gave it considerable prominence by featuring it en tour through Maine and Massachusetts.[10]

This brief statement is made without any date or year mentioned. It is possible that Edwards' sources did not have the information available at the time they were consulted, or possibly that Hall's contribution to the American Cadet Band was considered so slight by Portland musicians that the year was unimportant.[11]

In Portland, Hall had to make his reputation all over again, and once again he relied on his ability as a cornetist. The Waterville public was still hungry for news of their popular band leader, and the *Waterville Mail* obliged with the following clipping from the Portland Press.

In speaking of the third annual concert and ball given by the American Cadet Band of Portland, Wednesday Evening, the first appearance of the band under the leadership of Prof. R. B. Hall, the Portland Press says:

From 8: o'clock to 9: o'clock the band under their new leader Mr. R. B. Hall played a number of selections exceedingly well. It was reserved for Mr. Hall, however, to arouse the enthusiasm of his audience by his brilliant rendering of Hartmann's Concert Polka, on his gold cornet. His execution was fine, and he obtained an admirable tone from his instrument. He received a hearty encore.[12]

Hall's conspicuous absence from the Waterville press is ended the following spring on April first with a short piece in the *Mail* . Once again feelers must have been being made to see if Hall could be induced to return to Waterville, even though this is not what the paper actually said.

The prospect for a reorganization of the Waterville Military Band seems rather dubious. It was thought some time ago that it would be possible to get the band going as this is to be a presidential year and there will be more than the usual amount of work for a band in this section of the state. The MAIL learns, however, that several of the best players in the old band have left the city during the winter and that several more will leave during the summer, so that but a fragment of the former organization will be left. It is too bad that this city must lose so good a band, and it is annoying to reflect that it is partly because of a lack of appreciation that this state of things has come. A little more liberality on the part of the citizens would have kept Mr. R. B. Hall here and with him at the head of the band it would have been maintained as one of the best in the state, a source of enjoyment to the public and pride to the city.[13]

Ever the champion of the band's cause, the *Mail* once again took the citizens to task for failing to afford Hall's keep. A good band was important to the city in terms of attracting commerce and industry, an important aspect of the era's inter-city rivalry. Whether or not Hall had been in contact with the editors or other Waterville friends prior to this, the piece did serve to stir up interest in getting Hall back again, as the following week's *Mail* points out.

A member of the Waterville Military Band that was, informs THE MAIL that an effort is being made to reorganize the band for the coming summer. He says that a large number of business men, now that there is a prospect of having no band in the city, are becoming interested in the matter and express themselves as ready to contribute to the band's support. It is rumored, too, that the health of Mr. Hall, the former leader, now at the head of the American Cadet Band of Portland, is not very good, and that he might possibly be induced to return here if the right sort of support could be guaranteed the Waterville organization.[14]

Having printed a rumor, the editors deserved a good denial, and the following week they were forced to eat their words, even if only temporarily.

Prof. R. B. Hall informs the Portland Press that there is nothing in the report that he intends to return to Waterville. The Press adds that it is pleasant to know that so good a musician as R. B. Hall is well satisfied with his home there.[15]

Sometimes a prompt denial only confirms the truth of a rumor, and that was apparently the case in this affair. Negotiations with Hall were obviously in progress. The following week a small item indicated that the

Waterville Military Band was being reorganized, and that Mr. Whittier would act as leader. Civic pride as much as any other motivation was behind the effort, and the *Mail* reported that "many citizens feel that it is not becoming to a city like Waterville not to have a band."[16]

A week later success was at hand; Hall had been persuaded to return to Waterville. The announcement of this happy event in the *Mail* is worth quoting for the detail it gives on Hall's return, his value to the community, and the announcement of a subscription drive to pay for the band's reorganization. Once again Hall's health is an issue, as is the raising of a sufficient sum of money for his salary. The editors evidently considered this story to be very important because they placed it on page two, graced it with a headline and gave it a sub-headline, making much more of this news of Hall's return than the brief announcement on the local page that usually accompanied his doings.

THE OLD LEADER IS BACK

Prof. Hall to re-organize and again lead the Waterville Military Band.

It will be a very pleasant news for music lovers in this city and vicinity to learn that inducements have been offered sufficient to influence Prof. R. B. Hall, the noted composer of band music and cornet player, to return to Waterville and again take charge of the Waterville Military Band.

Prof. Hall was the original organizer of this band and for several years worked hard together with the members, to bring it to a point where it ranked with the very best bands in Maine. Indeed when Mr. Hall gave up the leadership there were only two or three bands that were in its class. Last fall Mr. Hall went to Portland to take charge of the American Cadet Band in that city.

Efforts have been made to return here but in spite of the fact that his health has not been so good in Portland as it was when he lived here, he has refused to come. Within a few days, however, negotiations have been set on foot as a result of which Mr. Hall will come at once and reorganize the band, and it is probable that within the next two weeks he will again be a resident of Waterville.

Mr. Hall has been greatly missed. Waterville people had grown used to hearing fine band music and it was a deprivation not at all pleasant to have it taken away. They will be glad to have it back again. Right here a word of prompting might not be out of place.

It is a well known fact that it costs money to maintain a good band and there isn't enough band work in this vicinity to make a band self-supporting. The only way then in which the city can have a fine band is by contributions on the part of citizens, together with what aid the city council might see fit to grant. That should be borne in mind when the man with a subscription paper comes around. It isn't safe for a man to trust his neighbor to subscribe what is needed. He should put his own name down.[17]

The editors of the *Mail* were anxious to have Hall back, and enthusiastic about the band. It is interesting that even in a paper intended only for a local Waterville public, they took every opportunity to puff the band's reputation under Hall. The *Mail* valued the band as a community asset.

The entire last paragraph of this story was devoted to the idea of a fund drive for the band. For the *Mail*, funding was the key issue in maintaining a good band, because without money they were sure to lose the services of their valued leader. Two winters in a row Hall had left Waterville for greener pastures, only to return because of health concerns. The pleading and promises of local friends that brought him back would be to no avail if the money could not be raised to fulfill those promises. He had been ill in February of 1894 even in Waterville, but obviously felt that he fared even worse in larger cities. Without medical records it cannot be said for sure whether Hall suffered from true consumption, today commonly called tuberculosis, which was rampant in the cities prior to the turn of the century. Whatever the cause, he seemed to do better in Waterville than elsewhere.

Hall's reputation throughout the state was such that his move from Portland to Waterville was even news in Bangor. The following article was republished in the *Waterville Mail* in its "From Other Papers" column, a section usually reserved for subjects of a political or sensational nature. Here the *Mail* quotes the *Bangor Daily Commercial*:

Bangor Commercial— Portland has lost a polished composer and musician in the person of R. B. Hall who has been the leader of the American Cadet Band of that city for some time. This end came about by the numerous earnest solicitations of the musical people of Waterville, where he has gone to resume his directorship of the Waterville Military Band.

The Portland Band while regretting the loss of Mr. Hall, are very much gratified to know that he has a worthy successor, Mr. Charles Schonland, a worthy musician in every sense of the word, and a man who can make a sausage just as good as he can play a cornet.[18]

By juxtaposing those two short paragraphs, the Bangor editor has pointed out, in keeping with the undertones of inter-city rivalry and competitive spirit of the day, the irony of the state's largest city losing a composer, and replacing him with a butcher. The *Mail* in reprinting it acknowledged the compliment being paid by the Queen City's press for Waterville's victory in the exchange. The message for the modern reader is that bands in that era were an important vehicle in inter-city rivalry.

By mid-May, 1896, Hall had returned for at least one rehearsal of the Waterville Military Band, and the *Mail* stated that "the members were pleased to welcome their old leader back."[19] Now fully reorganized, the band's size had increased to twenty-five members. The *Mail* listed the instrumentation as follows: "Six cornets, one piccalo [sic], one E-flat clarionet, four B-flat clarionets, three altos, one horn, one euphonium, four trombones, two basses, drum and cymbals."[20] This instrumentation is significant for anyone performing or analyzing

Hall's marches of this period, because it indicates the balance available for rehearsing prior to publication. It also explains the absence of saxophone and flute parts, except when added by the publishers. An undated photograph of the Waterville Military Band which appeared in the Waterville Sentinel Sesquicentennial Supplement shows the band at a strength of twenty, the instrumentation as noted above, except only one clarinet and fewer alto horns.[21]

The following week Hall released a few quotes to the Waterville paper, and his statements about more popular programming for the summer concerts were obviously aimed at improving responses to the subscription drive being started by his friends.

Prof. R. B. Hall says that the Waterville Military Band is in condition to play better this summer than ever before. Several new pieces have been added to the band lately and the men are already in very good practice. When the open air concerts are commenced the people may expect to hear much better music than they did last year. Mr. Hall says that he intends to play more of the popular pieces of the class of music this summer which seems to meet the approval of the people better who attend the open air concerts and he promises to give the people just what they want. Mr. Hall will move back here and make his home in the city as formerly.[22]

Noteworthy in this announcement is the concept that the band was expected to be dormant in the winter months, reviving for the open air season. The addition of "pieces" (by which is meant additional players and their instruments, rather than additional musical selections) and the reflection that "the men are already in very good practice" seems to indicate that rehearsals had been in progress even longer than the previous two weeks. The emphasis on popular programming and audience-pleasing indicates that this may be a change from the previous season, and is something that park bands go through periodically even to this day. The reiteration that "Hall says" indicates that the item was given to the paper by Hall himself, as an attempt to reawaken interest in the band among the potential audience, and, as the following week's editorial bears out, potential donors.

Hall had spent the winter of '95 in Albany, and the band fair had been under the management of a replacement. The summer's activities (1895) had been less rewarding than usual; even though a city appropriation had been made, there had been no subscription campaign. The coffers of the band were fairly depleted, which meant a smaller budget and a smaller and less active band.

Then, during the winter of '95-'96, Hall had been in Portland. In the spring there had been no band fair in Waterville, and all funding for the coming season would have to depend on the subscription drive. Perhaps Hall had learned while in Albany a greater appreciation of the power of the press to garner attention, audience, and ultimately money for his band; it took a year of hard times to bring it out in Waterville.

Even though the editors of the *Mail* were staunch supporters of the band and believers in summer concerts for Waterville, Hall's statements were important to give authenticity to the paper's editorializing about the fund campaign. Just one week later the *Mail* ran a fairly long editorial boosting the band and R. B. Hall, and announcing a fund drive to support the concerts:

A subscription paper has been started to secure funds for a series of open air concerts by the Waterville Military Band during the coming months. For several years these concerts have been a source of pleasure to a large number of citizens and it is to be hoped that those called upon will contribute liberally. The Waterville band is one of the best in the state and the people are very glad to see Mr. R. B. Hall

at the head again. In order to keep the band together, however, and to enable Mr. Hall to relocate here it is necessary to raise some money. The work that falls to a band in a city of this size is not sufficient to keep it going, and the deficit must be made up by popular subscriptions and what money is raised by the city. We have no doubt that the present city council will vote a sum of money for the concerts this summer as in former years, but that will not render it any less necessary that a good sum be raised by subscription. Let us treat the band well for it is a good one and a credit to the city.[23]

This informative editorial is especially interesting for the light it sheds on the band's affairs (and Hall's) during this era. In appealing for funds the paper makes it plain that Hall had been gone from the city, that the band had been without his services, and that the issue was money to provide for the band and for Hall. It is also stated as obvious that the paying work the band could expect was sparse enough so that both city funding and private contributions were necessary if a high quality organization were to be maintained.

Combined with the previous week's piece on the band, it is apparent that the quality and popularity of the band had slipped in Hall's absence, and that his return was not such a sure thing, but depended on adequate financing. As much as the previous week's article seemed to be fed to the paper by Hall, this editorial has a local bias, and seems to originate at the editor's desk.

Hall and the Waterville Military Band were already busily seeking those extra paid engagements, however, and one of them was playing for Memorial Day in Kents Hill. Because the Band had already been engaged to play in Waterville's Memorial Day Parade on the 30th, which was a Saturday, and also for an evening concert, after the Grand Army of the Republic ceremonies, this meant a very busy day for the band. A quick train ride following the dirge at the end of Waterville's parade was to be followed by an afternoon parade and ceremony at Kents Hill and another quick train ride back to Waterville for the evening concert.[24] This would not be an extraordinary feat for a band nowadays, using automobiles or a bus, but a century ago when transportation was more cumbersome it must have involved some close timing.

The same day, the Newport band was playing for Fairfield's Memorial Day, in spite of the fact that the Fairfield band had just been revived and was now up to 18 members.[25] To put these events in perspective, this was the week that the first coin operated telephones were installed in the Waterville train station, and only fifteen years after the very first telephones had been installed at central locations in Maine towns and cities. Advertising and city directories indicate that a few individuals and about a fourth of businesses had telephones by this time.

According to a short announcement the following week, Hall had not been chosen for the Colby commencement, an event with which he was later to become so strongly associated that it was mentioned prominently in his obituary and subsequent writings about his career. The Second Regiment Band of Lewiston had been selected to perform.[26]

Hall had not been involved in the previous year's Colby commencement either, probably in greatest part because of his absence from the city. He had been in Albany one year and Portland the next, during the winter and early spring when such decisions were made.

The following week a concert series tour was announced by Given's Orchestral Club of Portland, which had engaged R. B. Hall as cornet soloist for a week's trip to western Maine summer venues including Fryeburg, Bridgton, Farmington, and Buxton. Hall was a soloist who could attract crowds even to a small orchestra anywhere in Maine.[27]

Although July Fourth passed without any mention of the band's activities the *Mail* published a short appreciative note pertaining to the regular weekly concert on Tuesday, July 7.

The usual large crowd assembled for the band concert Tuesday evening and listened with keen pleasure to the fine selections rendered. The audience compelled the musicians to give two extra numbers at the close of the programme. It was a delightful evening for the concert — too warm to sit indoors but cool and comfortable in the park.[28]

This brief review does not mention Hall by name, nor does it name the band or any of the selections. The public knew what band had played, who had conducted, and either already knew or didn't much care which pieces had been played. The perspective of the *Mail* was that this was simply a pleasant entertainment for a warm evening. The noteworthy feature of the review is that it was printed at all. Regular Tuesday summer concerts had been occurring for years, and would occur for many more years, often without notice of any sort in the press. It may not be making too much of it to say that the Waterville public's interest in the band was at a peak during the summer of 1896.

As a rule during these years the *Mail* neither published announcements of the weekly band concerts nor reviewed them. The excitement of the earlier era when band concerts had been a new thing was long past. Only when there was a change was notice taken. In this way we often learn of Hall's activities beyond the normal schedule of concerts. Such is the following notice of a postponement.

On account of the absence from town of several members of the band there was no concert last evening. It will be given on Friday evening of this week instead. Prof. Hall is in Fryeburg and four of the players are playing with the Fairfield [band] at the Catholic fair in that town.[29]

The same paper includes an announcement of Col. George A. Philbrook's recent visit to the city. Commander of the Second Regiment of the National Guard, State of Maine, Philbrook periodically came to Waterville to review the local Company H. A social evening was usually held after the inspection, often with band music, or an orchestra and dancing, which made the visits an event for the musicians as well as the militia.

Col. George A. Philbrook of the Second Regiment paid an official visit to Co. H of this city Friday night.... The men were assembled at an early hour as as soon as

Col. Philbrook was ready inspection was ordered.... Col Philbrook is a gentlemanly man and the boys always enjoy a visit from him. Friday night was no exception to that rule.[30]

Hall's march *Col. Philbrook* was published by Carl Fischer in 1894, and was intended for this Col. Philbrook rather than Waterville attorney Hon. Warren C. Philbrook. W. C. Philbrook was State Assistant Attorney General, Mayor of Waterville, Associate Justice of the Maine Supreme Court, an amateur musician, and a friend of Hall, but never a Colonel.

Ever an advocate for the band's cause, the *Mail* ran a long editorial in the same issue, again arguing for a city appropriation to support the band. Citing the demise of the Bath and Gardiner bands as an example, the editors make a case for the need to pay band members as follows:

Bath and Gardiner are both wishing for a return of the good old days when some musical genius gathered together the musical talent of the town into a band that gave credit to the place. They may well wish in vain. The days when bands were maintained simply because the members loved music is past. Men nowadays are too busy to give up their time and practice without some material return for the same.

There aren't enough engagements in the ordinary country towns to support a good band and the only way to make possible the existence of such an organization is for the town or city to make an appropriation for concerts to be furnished by the band, or else for individuals who are interested to put their hands in their pockets and help pay the expenses of the band.[31]

Obviously, the plight of the town band has been a problem for a very long time. If the music is to be good, able and intelligent people must commit large amounts of practice and rehearsal time, and an exemplary individual must be found to lead them. The dictates of modern life make financial reward necessary to sustain this kind of an effort. Pure volunteerism often peters out after a brief run of enthusiasm, and the band heads into decline unless members and leaders are paid. Ultimately, sponsors or contributors must make up the deficit engendered by such an operation, or city money must be appropriated. The chief problem in sustaining a band has always been: who pays for it?

This very issue is at the center of Hall's professional career. The pursuit of a better living from music took him from Richmond to Boston; to Bangor; to roaming the state teaching various bands; to Waterville; to Albany; and to Portland, from which his health ultimately drove him back to

Waterville. All this in quest of an opportunity to organize a good band, well supported, with fair recompense for the leader.

A final announcement from the summer of 1896 indicates a kind of band activity which Hall was known to enjoy. In Charlie Wakefield's words:

"Hall was a great hand to go on excursions."[32]

As the *Waterville Mail* notes:

Next Sunday the Waterville Military Band will give a sacred concert at Maranacook. A special train will be run from Skowhegan and intermediate stations leaving here about 9 o'clock in the morning with the fare placed at the low price of 75 cents for the round trip.[33]

Excursions were a mainstay for the bands of that era, and the Waterville Military Band was no exception. As had been the case with the Bangor Band and its public, Kineo, Maranacook, Northport, Belfast, Fort Popham, Boothbay, all were popular destinations. From Waterville, however, mid-coast destinations were closer, and Penobscot Bay destinations were farther, involving a longer train—rather than boat—trip. From Richmond or Bath one could take a steamer excursion to Fort Popham, including a boat ride to Seguin and Boothbay, and return, complete with rail passage from Richmond back to Waterville, all in a weekend package. Rates were low enough so that ordinary people could make these trips, and did in large numbers. A band was frequently part of the festivities, and played on the train ride or boat ride as well as for dancing at the destination. A band concert was often part of the program, along with the clambake and dancing or entertainment.

Clubs, lodges, and organizations made such trips a mainstay of their annual programs, and public excursions were organized and advertised for most weekends in the good weather season. At other times of the year, package tours would take people from points along the rail line, on a special train to hear a concert such as the Gilmore or Sousa Band in Portland or Bangor and include tickets, hotel, train fare, and sometimes even a pre- or post-concert dinner, in the package price.

The Waterville Military Band often went on such excursions, usually hired by the organizers, but occasionally in later years sponsoring their own trips to Kineo. There the band went and played for pleasure, and others went along to follow the music, by paying their own way ultimately subsidizing the Band's outing.

Band Concert Poster, October 8, 1896. (Courtesy Bagaduce Music Lending Library, Blue Hill, Maine).

This poster shows the Band's program for an October agricultural fair in the western Maine town of Canton. Once again the Waterville Military Band was dormant during the winter months of 1896-97, following familiar pattern of giving up band work once cold weather arrived,and favoring orchestra and theater work until it was time to revive the band in the spring. The *Mail* reported this as news of the new season, with the usual plea for support.

There was a large attendance at the rehearsal of the Waterville Military Band Thursday evening, and the music was played in a manner that bespeaks credit for the organization and its leader, Prof. R. B. Hall. The band work has been somewhat neglected during the Winter on account of the large amount of work which the Orchestra has had, but by the six or eight rehearsals which have been held during the past few weeks, it is evident that the band will open the spring campaign in the best condition it ever has as far as its musical capacity is concerned. It now remains for the people of this City to support the organization as it deserves.[34]

The following week an Easter concert for the benefit of the band was announced, and all were urged to buy a ticket to support the band. Sadly, though, in the review the subsequent week only a modest attendance was reported.

In spite of the fine program and quality renditions it was a financial flop for the band.[35]

The remainder of the 1897 season passed very quietly for the band. The usual park concerts were given, but little extra work was reported, and the press became increasingly interested in the efforts of New York musical director William Rogers Chapman to organize and site the Maine Music Festival. First mounted in 1897, the Maine Music Festival became an annual event with concerts in Portland and Bangor on successive weeks for thirty years until 1926. In conjunction with the Festival, Chapman organized the Maine Symphony Orchestra, in which R. B. Hall played first cornet from its inception until his final illness.[36]

In 1897, Hall, too, was caught up in the excitement of the first Maine Music Festival. He played in the orchestra under the baton of Chapman, who was also, for a time, conductor of the New York Philharmonic. Here he had an opportunity to perform great masterpieces of the standard orchestral repertoire, operatic excerpts from all the most popular operas with internationally famous soloists brought to Maine from New York, and great oratorios.

In the first Maine Music Festival more than fifty such works were performed. Often some movements of a longer work were performed on one evening, and others on subsequent programs, so that a whole symphony would be heard as a part of three or four programs. A partial listing of works performed either in excerpt or in their entirety at that first festival includes Handel's *Messiah*, Mendelssohn's *Elijah*, Mozart's *Mass in C-minor*, Rossini's *Stabat Mater*, Schubert's *Symphony in C Major*, Beethoven's *Eighth Symphony*, and Raff's *Symphony No. 5*. Operatic selections that first year included excerpts from Wagner's *Die Meistersinger von Nürnberg*, *Tannhäuser*, *Tristan und Isolde*, and *Lohengrin*; Verdi's *Il Trovatore*; Leoncavallo's *I Pagliacci*; Gounod's *Faust,* and *Romeo and Juliette*; Weber's *Oberon*; Donizetti's *Lucia di Lammermoor*, (the famous sextette, of course); Bizet's *Carmen*; Rossini's *William Tell*; and many, many more excerpts from similar operas. Maine day at the Festival featured works by Maine composers Andrews, Kotzschmer, Silsby, and others, and pieces by the Festival's organizer and director, Chapman.

The following year Hall wrote his *Maine Festival March*, which was "dedicated to Mr. Wm. R. Chapman," and played at the 1898 Maine Festival under the heading of "Works By Maine Composers."[37]

By participating in these festivals, Hall had the opportunity to perform more than fifty standard pieces and a dozen works by Maine contemporaries every year. Even allowing for repeats of certain favorites from year to year, several hundred items of the orchestral and operatic repertoire were covered during the eight years (1897-1904) that Hall played in the orchestra. From the programs, we know that Hall played the important Beethoven, Brahms, Schubert, and Tschaikowsky symphonies. We likewise know that when he led the Waterville Military Band in selections from *Les Hugénots*, *Le Prophète*, *Martha*, or *Faust*, for example, that he knew what the orchestrations and vocal parts sounded like, not just the band arrangements. When Hall, the composer, included a passing reference to *Lohengrin*, in the break-strain of his 1900 march Commonwealth, we know that he had indeed played that piece in the preceding year. Even though only four notes are quoted, they are such a distinct "leit-motif" that there is no doubt Hall expected his audience to be reminded of the famous fanfare from Wagner's immensely popular opera.

We also know from these programs that Maine's musical public was exposed to these great masterpieces on a continuing basis. A chorus of well over a thousand was raised each year. Chapman had specially prepared vocal scores of the choral numbers published, and the choruses rehearsed in their own localities throughout the year, before gathering for the week of rehearsals that preceded the festival. With five nights of performances in Portland (each performance was a different program) followed by five more performances in Bangor, more than fifty thousand admission tickets were sold each year.

The Maine Music festivals were to be a continuing part of Hall's life during the ensuing years as he built up the Waterville Military Band, and added to his ever increasing creative output of fine marches.

March Commonwealth by R. B. Hall, measures 78-80 of the solo cornet part, showing the bass cue notes.[38]

NOTES

1 *Waterville* [Maine] *Mail* , 22 March 1895. (Hereafter, *WM*).

2 *WM*, 5 April 1895.

3 *WM*, 12 April 1895.

4 *WM*, 19 April 1895.

5 *WM*, 17 May 1895.

6 It must have been quite a sight seeing Hall marching with a crutch or a cane on his arm, sometimes playing the solo cornet part an octave higher than written. Playing the lead an octave higher was a technique attributed to several cornet virtuosi of that era, and was so much a part of the popular perception of the turn-of-the-century band leader that it was eventually immortalized in the lyrics of Meredith Willson's "Seventy-six Trombones" from *The Music Man*.

7 These weekly programs are among the very few of Hall's programs that have survived; little ephemera of this nature survived the century in Waterville.

8 *WM*, 2 August 1895.

9 *WM*, 11 October 1895, 3.

10 George Thornton Edwards, *Music and Musicians of Maine*, (Portland, Maine: Southworth Press, 1928), 334-335.

11 Edwards gives a full and detailed treatment to about twenty-five bands of this era, including a relatively complete history of both the Bangor Band and Chandler's Band of Portland. He makes no mention whatever of the Waterville Military Band. Similarly, he relegates Hall to passing references such as the one quoted above, omitting him entirely from both the biography section and the Maine composers section of his otherwise authoritative volume. This passage is the only one in which Edwards mentions Hall as a composer.

12 *WM*, 1 November 1895, 3.

13 *WM*, 1 April 1896, 5.

14 *WM*, 8 April 1896, 5.

15 *WM*, 15 April 1896.

16 *WM*, 29 April 1896.

17 *WM*, 6 May 1896, 2.

18 *WM*, 10 June 1896.

19 *WM*, 13 May 1896, 5.

20 Ibid.

21 *Waterville* [Maine] *Morning Sentinel*, City of Waterville Sesquicentennial edition, 19 July 1952.

22 *WM*, 20 May 1896, 4.

23 *WM*, 27 May 1896, 4.

24 *WM*, 27 May 1896, 3 June 1896.

25 *WM*, 20 May 1896, 3 June 1896.

26 *WM*, 3 June 1896.

27 *WM*, 10 June 1896.

28 *WM*, 8 July 1896.

29 *WM*, 29 July 1896.

30 *WM*, 29 July 1896.

31 *WM*, 29 July 1896, 4.

32 NA#2261.069.

33 *WM*, 29 July 1896.

34 *WM*, 7 April 1897.

35 *WM*, 21 April 1897.

36 Edwards, *Music and Musicians of Maine*, 221-223,378.

37 *Programs of the Maine Music Festivals, 1897-1904*, ("Published by the Management." no city, np. nd.). This volume, and the entire collection of lavishly illustrated annual program booklets, can be seen at Special Collections, Raymond Fogler Library, University of Maine, Orono, Maine.

38 R. B. Hall, *Commonwealth*, (Cincinnati, Ohio: John Church, 1900), m. 78-79. One additional cue note was added for clarity in this example.

CHAPTER EIGHT
PEAK YEARS WITH THE WATERVILLE MILITARY BAND (1897-1905)

The seasons of 1897 and 1898 passed quietly for the Waterville Military Band. The usual summer concerts were given, the usual difficulty in raising money was noted, although press attention to the band was less frequent than it had been in previous years. The city appropriated a small sum for the sustenance of the band, and an annual subscription helped to provide a salary for the leader that, though meager, was just enough to keep him from leaving again. Hall was busy in Chapman's Maine Symphony through the summer and fall each year, and was involved in Hall's Orchestra for dance engagements which apparantly had replaced Dinsmore's as well as "The Waterville Military Band Orchestra" in Hall's customary occupation. He also appeared with other orchestras such as Haley's or Pullen's, and was a frequent soloist with other bands throughout the state, especially in Belfast and Lewiston.

During this time Hall had a large number of students, and taught on many other instruments besides the cornet.[1] The Waterville City Directory for 1897-98 contains a quarter page advertisement for "Robert B. Hall, Music Teacher," giving the address as his rooms at 168 Main Street, Waterville.[2] It was during this time that Hall began teaching Arthur Roundy, and eventually bought him his first good clarinet, a Buffet, so that Roundy could join the band. Roundy paid him back over time from his band earnings, two dollars at a time.[3] The lessons at that time were 75 cents.[4]

Although they were relatively quiet seasons for the band, these were active years for R. B. Hall as a composer, with John Church publishing at least two of his marches in each of the two years. Church's publications were *Hamiltonian*, and *American Belle*, in 1897; and *Philo Senate* and *Charge of the Battalion*, in 1898. Additionally, during this time Hall was composing (and rehearsing with the Waterville Military Band) some of the marches that were to be published later, or even posthumously. The town of Randolph was incorporated in 1897, leading to Hall's *Randolph*, published in 1899; the *Maine*

Festival March, which was performed at the Maine Music Festival in October of 1898, was published by Church in 1899. Hall's busy association with Philadelphia music publisher Harry Coleman was represented during this period with only one offering, a *Song for Cornet or Trombone* (Coleman, 1897) although some of Rehrig's evidence suggests that Coleman engraved many of the marches that were then published by Fischer, Church, or others.[5]

In 1899 events in Waterville precipitated another financial crisis that generated newspaper attention and publicity for Hall and the band. Although the band's finances were more bleak than in the past two years, with city money in short supply, the band was still very popular with the Waterville citizenry, and Hall was a local celebrity. In spite of the fact that Hall's long time associate, Judge W. C. Philbrook, had been elected mayor, the City Council eliminated the small appropriation for the band's concerts. Once again the editors of the *Waterville Mail* took up the cudgel in the band's behalf, and began to call for increased public support.

By early June, 1899, the band season had not yet begun, and the issue of whether Hall would be engaged was very much in doubt. On June 7, the *Mail* ran two separate editorials on the issue.

It is announced that a canvass is to be made this week for the raising of a subscription fund for the Waterville Military Band.... Everybody enjoys the Summer concerts and it would be some very dull weeks without them, but neither a good band nor weekly summer concerts can be had unless money is forthcoming to support the band organization. There is not at present business enough of the ordinary sort to keep a band in existence here and the lack must be made up by those who enjoy the music if we are to have a band at all.[6]

This short piece is the usual plea for a subscription fund, and as such is not remarkable. Almost every year since Hall returned from Albany such a subscription had to be taken, and the paper promoted it in almost the same words. What is unusual here is the lateness of the season. The band should have begun by then, and the season should have been about to start. As the next editorial makes plain, Hall was balking until money could be raised.

Waterville lovers of band music will have a chance to declare themselves this week on the subject of retaining the services of Prof. R. B. Hall the coming year as instructor of the Military Band. Several business men of the city have voiced their willingness to subscribe liberally toward the necessary funds, and also to their readiness to present the matter in a clear way to others in a position to aid in a worthy cause. A subscription paper will be the means used and this will be circulated among the citizens during the coming week. Evening band concerts in past seasons have begun about the middle of June and the funds to support the same have been raised in advance.

Prof. Hall is known to have intimated that he will close his duties in this city, so far as the Band is concerned, by July 1, if the support, heretofore given him, does not materialize during the present month.[7]

However nicely the editors put it, this was an ultimatum. Hall had taken the unusual step of publicly announcing a date by which he would end his relationship with the Waterville Military Band if his supporters could not come forward with funds. Fortunately for Hall, funding did materialize, though not by July 1. Though the Waterville Military Band did not fizzle entirely that summer, the concerts were late to start, and most of the band's activity was in the form of excursions. Hall, meanwhile was busy as a soloist with other bands.

On June 21 the editors took the city council to task over their refusal to vote positively on the proposal for the Waterville Military Band:

It is hard to understand why the order providing for the giving of $150 to the Waterville Military Band for a series of summer night concerts on Monument Park should have been killed in the common council after it had received a passage in the board of aldermen. The members of the council who thought they were listening to the dictates of economy in voting against the order should remember that these concerts are enjoyed by thousands of citizens, and that there aren't a dozen taxpayers in the city who would refuse to help pay their fair share of the extra burden entailed by this appropriation.... Let's have them as we have had them in the past.[8]

It is a measure of both the Band's popularity and the paper's clout that the next month's council meeting reversed this exercise in political penury, and passed the appropriation for the band.[9] The assertion that the concerts were "enjoyed by thousands" is a particularly important remark. Every time the band gave a summer night open-air concert, large and enthusiastic audiences were on hand. The summer concerts began almost immediately, since the band was ready and had been playing excursions, but it was a much later than usual start for the Waterville Military Band's summer season.

During this time of indecision, Hall had begun casting an eye toward the directorship of the National Soldiers Home Band at Togus, which had a relatively large and good band under the direction of Prof. Berthold W. Thieme. Thieme was a cornet player and teacher from Germany who had had a career in Boston before coming to Togus in the middle 1880's. It was a full-time salaried Veteran's Administration job, and although Hall "tried to pull strings to get that job" at various times, he never succeeded in dislodging Thieme, who came to hate him for meddling.[10] As it was, Thieme held the Togus job for more than 44 years, into the mid-1920's.[11] In the summer of 1899 Thieme's Togus Band garnered large audiences and favorable reviews, and some of the Waterville Military Band members went to play there while waiting for the Waterville season to begin.[12]

Hall also was working on his hobby of woodworking, and invited a reporter from the *Mail* to his apartment to see the latest results of his cabinetmaking. The timing of this visit, and the resultant item in the paper, could provoke speculation as to whether Hall was merely making use of slack time or regarding this as a fall-back career if things became too slow in the music business, as the reporter seemed to hint. The cabinets must have been impressive: an effusive story appeared in the following week's paper.

Prof. R. B. Hall followed the trade of a cabinetmaker before he came to be an expert player on the cornet. He sandwiches his time nowadays. When practice upon his favorite instrument and writing new music grow monotonous, he takes his hammer in hand, steps to his bench, and starts in on some style of cabinet suitable for ornament as well as usefulness in the home. A friend was invited into his workshop Friday to examine two small cabinets in the process of making, and he found them both to be excellent pieces of handicraft. They stand about two feet high, are lined with sateen, and covered with plush, and when finished should add much to the decorations of Prof. Hall's apartments.[13]

Hall had made several small wooden boats as a youth for use in the Kennebec, and had made sailboats and a canoe that he used when he stayed at Kineo, on Moosehead Lake.[14] The photo on the following page, is of half-models made by Hall for boats that he later built. These models were restored and mounted on a pine placque by Ralph Gould in 1967.

Hall was said to be "as gifted in carpentry as he was in music."[15] He also had made the music cabinets, desks and built-in uniform cabinets that graced the band room at 93 Main Street, and housed the effects of the

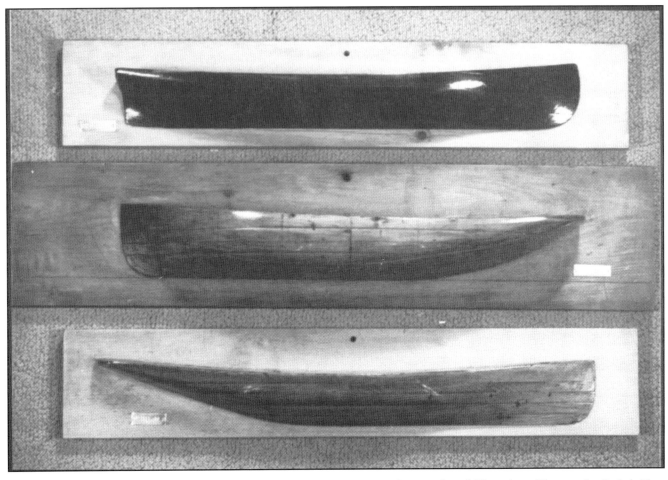

PLATE 9. HALF MODELS OF BOATS BUILT BY R. B. HALL, Restored and Placed on Placque by Ralph T. Gould (Courtesy of Bagaduce Music Lending Library)

news on August 2, with an excursion to Merrymeeting Park, at which Hall performed Missud's *Magnolia Serenade* as a cornet solo, and was so enthusiastically applauded that he was compelled to deliver an encore, Jordan's *The Song that Reached My Heart.*[17] But although it made the front page, which was unusual, the news itself was not out of the ordinary, for Hall was pressed for an encore practically every time he played.

The entire program was given on the newspaper's front page. Because it is one of the few excursion programs that has survived, it is quoted here.

Waterville Military Band.[16] It seems that when band work was slow, Hall could turn to cabinetmaking and carpentry, though (fortunately for musicians who continue to revere his music) this remained a hobby for him.

The remainder of the summer season of 1899 was relatively uneventful, once the financial impediment to the concert season was resolved. Hall and the Waterville Military Band made front page

A close inspection of this program indicates a generally light character to the selections, all crowd-pleasers similar to a park concert even today. Keler Bela's *Hungarian Lustspeil*, the Overture and the "heaviest" of the selections, is a light, acces-

March	Stars and Stripes	Sousa
Overture	Hungarian Lustspeil	Keler Bela
Waltz	Land of My Dreams	Herman
Cornet Solo (Prof. R. B. Hall)	Magnolia Serenade	Missud
Characteristic	Lime Kiln Club's Soiree	Laurendau
Medley	Popular Favorites	Beyer
Concert Waltz	Italian Nights	Tobani
March	Hamiltonian	R. B. Hall[18]

Text of the program for the August 2, 1899 concert performed at Merrymeeting Park, as quoted in the Waterville (Maine) Mail of that date.

sible piece and is frequently programmed by traditional park bands and enjoyed by summer audiences even to this day. Only two marches were played: Sousa's *The Stars and Stripes Forever*, which was relatively new then, but already a national favorite, as it has remained; and Hall's own *Hamiltonian*.

The same day, an announcement of Hall's forthcoming appearance on Sunday at Lakewood, "the New Excursion Resort," declared that the Waterville Military Band would give concerts "all day long." The other attractions for the excursionist were to include: "boating, bathing, fishing, deer park, fine collection of animals, etc., and picnics."[19] Hall and the Waterville Military Band were to return to Lakewood on many occasions during the next few summer seasons.

Hall spent the middle of August on tour in New Hampshire with Prof. William Rogers Chapman and the Maine Festival Orchestra (also called the Maine Symphony Orchestra).[20] The musical fare for these tours leaned heavily on orchestral classics and operatic excerpts. Programs were similar to those of the Maine Music Festivals held annually in Bangor and Portland, but without the huge chorus and with fewer New York soloists.

In September Hall appeared as soloist with the Lewiston Brigade Band at the State Fair. The Lewiston Brigade Band was also known at this time as the Second Regiment Band, having received the regimental appointment after the Bangor Band vacated it. A trombonist from Arkansas (who was un-named in the local papers, probably because he was not a local celebrity) was also featured on the program, which had been promoted as a "cornet-trombone dream" in advance announcements.[21]

Hall had with him the manuscript for his new march *Greeting to the Admiral* which received its premiere performance at the fair.[22] The title was "In anticipatory tribute to the homecoming of Admiral Dewey."[23] Dewey's arrival in Boston at the end of October was a celebrated and newsworthy event, though his tour didn't have much to do with Maine. It took him to Montpelier and

Northfield, Vermont, where he was received at Norwich Academy on November 1. The following year (1900), when Admiral Dewey's visit to New England was merely a memory, the march was published by John Church as *Commonwealth*, the title by which it is known today.

Waterville hosted a large gathering of Knights Templars in October, 1899, where they paraded for Saint Omer's Day, and were entertained by both the Bath Band and the Waterville Military Band. The concert, held at the Elmwood Hotel, is interesting because the bands each gave a complete, if short, concert program, although the *Mail* reported that they alternated pieces.[24] Hall had composed a march for the Knights Templars in Bath, *Dunlap Commandery*, but for some reason never entitled one for the Saint Omer Commandery in Waterville. That task was left to William D. Haines, Hall's successor with the Waterville Military Band and a disciple of his march writing style.

It is interesting to note that the Waterville Military Band programmed significantly longer and more serious numbers than did the Bath Band, whose selections were lighter and more like the program that the Waterville Military Band had played earlier at Merrymeeting Park. The Waterville band was

	Waterville Military Band	
March	Bay State Cmdry.	Burrell
Overture	Zampa	Herold
Selection	Faust	Gounod
Potpourri	German Comic Opera	Laurendau
Medley	The Winner	Meckle
March	Whistling Rufus	Mills
Cornet Solo (Prof. R. B. Hall)	Magnolia Serenade	Missud
encore (Prof. Hall)	The Song That Reached My Heart	Jordan

Waterville Military Band program for the concert at the Elmwood Hotel, October, 1899 as quoted in the Waterville (Maine) Mail, 18 October 1899.

at home, at full strength, and so could manage the longer and more complex selections, such as *Zampa* and *Faust*.

The Bath band, on the other hand, was traveling and stuck with sure-fire crowd pleasers even though they probably had some big selections in their repertoire. Hall's solo and encore were the same as they had been on the Merrymeeting Park excursion.

The remainder of 1899 passed quietly for Hall, with occasional appearances at the Knights of Pythias, Canton Halifax, and the Pittsfield I.O.O.F. lodge (Court Sebasticook, #33). His only publication that year was the Maine Festival March from John Church, which had been premiered at the previous year's Maine Festival in Bangor. The year's financial difficulties had taken their toll on the band, and Hall sought a

<table>
<tr><td colspan="3" align="center">*Bath Band*</td></tr>
<tr><td>*March*</td><td>*Dandy Fifth*</td><td>*Devlin*</td></tr>
<tr><td>*Descriptive*</td><td>*The Cuban Way*</td><td>*Dalbey*</td></tr>
<tr><td>*Cornet Solo*
(Mr. Raffael)</td><td>*The Sweetest Story Ever Told*</td><td>*Sulta*</td></tr>
<tr><td>*Waltz*</td><td>*Danube Waves*</td><td>*Grossinger*</td></tr>
<tr><td>*Reverie*</td><td>*Wayside Chapel*</td><td>*Wilson*</td></tr>
<tr><td>*Medley*</td><td>*Coon's Picnic*</td><td>*Laurendau*</td></tr>
<tr><td>*Medley*</td><td>*Out For a Lark*</td><td>*De Witt*[25]</td></tr>
</table>

Bath Band program for the concert at the Elmwood Hotel, October, 1899 as quoted in the Waterville (Maine) Mail, 18 October 1899.

more stable and lasting arrangement. As the sporadic season of 1899 waned, Hall got together with a few prominent business supporters of the band to develop an idea for permanent support for the band. A significant change in the funding for the Waterville Military Band was underway, and would be announced with the turn of the new year.

Hall's Orchestra of twelve pieces ushered in the new year with a concert and New Year's Ball on January 1, 1900, in Waterville, and R. B. Hall followed this with a solo appearance in Bangor on January 3. This was business as usual for the active musician, but a bombshell announcement in the *Waterville Mail* of Wednesday, January 3, 1900, signaled a change for the better in Hall's financial picture.

THE BAND'S A SURETY

Waterville Military Band Corporation Formed By Leading Citizens

A corporation to be known as Hall's Military Band was organized Saturday at the office of Davis and Soule under the general laws of the State of Maine with a capital stock of $25000. The directors of the corporation are Geo. K. Boutelle, F. C. Thayer, H. E. Judkins, Frank Reddington, C. F. Johnson, G. F. Terry, J. F. Hill, W. T. Haines, C. B. Stetson. Mr. Boutelle, treasurer, Mr. Davis, clerk, Dr. J. F. Hill is president, and Prof. Hall manager and musical director. at a meeting of the directors Monday forenoon at 10:30 o'clock at the office of Davis & Soule.

All services performed by the officers of the corporation will be without salary. The stock will be placed among the friends of the organization in the city at par value, commissions and rebates not to figure at all. Already $300 has been pledged to the corporation and the business-like basis upon which the new corporation stands has led numbers who appreciate the worth of such an organization as the Military Band to the city to pledge their hearty support in the cause of advocating its interests as the success of the band for 1900 is assured.

In a talk with Cyrus W. Davis, the prime mover in the formation of the corporation, a Mail reporter learned that Prof. R. B. Hall will act as manager and musical director of both the Band and orchestra and will make all contracts with parties desiring the services of either organization, subject to such provisions as the corporation has marked out for him. He will receive remuneration, along with the members of the band and orchestra for services rendered in the way of engagements for music.

All funds received from engagements will be turned over to the treasurer. When engagements have been filled Prof. Hall will give each player of either organization an order on the treasurer so that they can get their pay without delay, a distinct advance over the methods prevailing hitherto, with bills remaining unpaid for some time.

The formation of this corporation appears to put at rest for a time to come the idea that Prof. Hall will leave the city for more lucrative fields. He has a strong liking for Waterville as a field for the practice of his profession and the excellent results that have followed from his direction of the band and orchestra during the time he has been here is sufficient warrant for the strong support given him at this time in trying to make the Waterville Military

Band outstanding in musical circles throughout the state.[26]

In announcing the new corporation, the *Mail* also outlined some of the troubles that had been plaguing the Waterville Military Band in the recent season, and reiterated the ever-present threat that Hall might leave again. The directors included two doctors, two lawyers, one financial manager of the electric company, and at least one banker. All were important businessmen in the community, and gave the new organization a substantial underpinning that had been lacking in previous years. By the following week, the corporation had been recorded in Augusta, and a certificate had been issued. The capital stock was listed at $25,620.00, paid in. This was a substantial sum of money at that time, and served to attract considerable press attention to the band. As the *Mail* reported it, the band was renamed "Hall's Military Band."[27]

The official history of Waterville quoted the corporation's charter stating its purpose as "establishing and maintaining in the city of Waterville a band and orchestra." Written in 1902, this history explains the workings of Waterville's government departments and interrelated civic groups in thorough detail. It states that the corporation pays Hall a salary, and band members for each service. Of the corporation, the centennial history says: "It exists,

however, not for the purpose of making money, but for the support of a band that will be a credit to the city, as Hall's Military Band and orchestra certainly are.[28]

With the band's finances stabilized, and Hall's salary assured, the newspaper announcements no longer needed to chide the public for lack of support, nor announce fund-raising activities. The result was a lighter editorial tone, which was welcome, but fewer opportunities for editorials, resulting in slightly less publicity for the band. The band performed its regular functions, including the Memorial Day parade, summer concerts, and various outings and excursions. Hall's various solo engagements in Bangor, Belfast, Skowhegan, Lewiston, or elsewhere, were announced as usual.

In the springtime, when band activity was beginning again, the news of Hall's doings centered around a big I.O.O.F. field day which was sponsored by Canton Halifax, and held in Waterville in May. Chandler's band from Portland came for the parade, and represented the First Regiment of Patriarchs Militant, while Hall's band represented the Second Regiment.[29]

Hall's Band and Orchestra was engaged for the Colby commencement that year. In spite of the fact that later writers were to say that he had guest musicians from Boston, the names of the players were all Bangor men: Dr. Oscar E. Wasgatt, H. M. Pullen, Harold J. Sawyer, Harvey J. Woods, Edward C. Adams, and Eugene A. Haley, all of Bangor.[30] These men were all well known to Hall; he had played with Pullen's Orchestra on many occasions, and Sawyer, Adams, and Haley had all been with Hall a decade earlier in the Bangor Band and Andrews' Orchestra. Another generation was represented in this group, however. In Bangor in the 1880's Hall had played in Andrews' Orchestra with Dr. Oscar E. Wasgatt's father, Dr. Emery T. Wasgatt, and with Harvey J. Woods's father, Horace Woods.

Hall's marches were being more widely played with each passing season. Although he had originally published with regional publishers such as Mace Gay in Brockton, Massachusetts, he now was being published and distributed by large, national publishing houses such as Carl Fischer in New York and John Church in Cincinnati, Ohio.

In spite of his national publications, Hall was regarded by the Waterville public as a local phenomenon, a situation which the editors of the *Mail* took every opportunity to redress. Later that summer, the *Mail* ran a reprint from the Atobi, Kansas, *Globe,* to demonstrate to the Waterville public just how far the fame of their own home town

bandmaster had spread. A lengthy summary of a concert program, featuring two of Hall's better known and more widely played marches, *Greeting to Bangor* and *Gardes du Corps*, is given and the following program note is reprinted:

GARDES DU CORPS

Written by a modest band master in Maine, R. B. Hall. Many regard him as the best march writer in America, but he is a genius who has never made money although his marches are played and admired everywhere.[31]

The *Mail* then continues the story of the concert, and concludes: "The many friends of Prof. Hall living in this section of the country will surely be interested to know how he is regarded far from home."[32]

A final note for the year (1900) underscores the band's importance to the community when, after the election results were announced, the winning Republican party hired Hall's Band, and a special electric streetcar to take the band, playing, up and down the trolley line all evening. The band was as important a part of the celebration as the torchlight parade and the victory bonfire. The reporter waxed eloquent in closing with: "The band played on, the horns tooted, and the red fire burned."[33]

The following year, 1901, Hall was as busy as ever with musical activities in Waterville. Although the Military Band was dormant through the winter and early spring, engagements began again at the end of April. Some writers have contended that Hall was in Albany, New York, for eleven months during this period, but no evidence exists in Albany to support that assertion, and news accounts clearly place Hall in Waterville for the entire period.

Continuing a pattern that had started in 1897 and became a six year trend, Hall's publishers brought out two marches in 1901. This year's publications were *Marche Funebre*, from Harry Coleman and Carl Fischer, and *The New Colonial*, which was published by John Church in the edition we know today, although an earlier edition of the same title had been previously credited to Carl Fischer in 1895. *Marche Funebre* is a funeral dirge of great beauty, and is used to this day by the United States Navy Band for the funerals of its highest ranking and most honored dead, and for the funerals of United States Presidents. *The New Colonial* is one of Hall's most elaborate parade marches, and is frequently played by the bigger and better bands.

At the end of April, 1901, the *Mail* ran a story outlining a contract dispute between Hall and the "Waterville

Military Band Association." That there was a dispute at all is not surprising, as times were hard in Waterville. Money was so tight that the plans and foundation for the new city hall were not paid for; the project was halted and abandoned until the architect sued the city.[34] Suddenly "Hall's Military Band Corporation" became, at least in the parlance of the newspaper, "The Waterville Military Band Association." This is startling and bespeaks a bitter disagreement between Hall and his supporters. Hall and the Association "differed in some particulars" but eventual resolution was foreseen by the editors.[35]

The contract must have been settled favorably, and fast, for the *Mail* never mentioned it again, and band news was positive in tone heading into the Memorial Day parade and the Patriarchs Militant field day. The band was referred to as the "Waterville Military Band" about twice as often as it was called "Hall's Band" in the *Mail*, although the terms were obviously regarded as interchangeable. The name "Hall's Military Band" was also equivalent, but came into use far less frequently. Despite the fact that the confusion about the name for the band persisted for nearly seventy-five years, no one at the time seemed to doubt what band was being discussed. R. B. Hall and the Waterville Military Band led the parade this year, instead of following the police and postal workers as usual, and performed at the afternoon ceremonies as

well.[36] The Patriarchs Militant field day was held in Bangor the following week; Chandler's Band of Portland represented the First Regiment, the Bangor Band represented the Second Regiment, and Hall's Band represented the Massachusetts Regiment. This was characterized as "a fine collection of bands."[37]

Hall's Band was engaged for the Colby commencement this year, and gave a Wednesday evening concert with a full band of twenty-five pieces. The *Mail* was laudatory in its review, beginning with the words: "Better music has perhaps never been given at a Colby commencement," and crediting the results to "the skilled direction of Prof. R. B. Hall."[38] The program consisted entirely of standard band fare of the day: transcriptions, a popular medley, and a patriotic medley. There were no marches, and none of Hall's original music was presented.[39] Text of the program appears on the following page.

The summer concerts in the park were held as usual, and as in most years the *Mail* did not print programs. The Waterville Military Band had its usual busy summer of excursions to Lakewood, Maranacook, Kineo, and elsewhere.

A single event dominated the summer's local news: progress on the troubled and delayed construction of the new city hall.

After funding denials and law suits, work on the building had finally been resumed. On Wednesday, August 21, 1901, the cornerstone for the new city hall was laid "with full Masonic ceremonies." Saint Omer's Commandery K. T. and the Waterville Lodge No. 33 F. & A. M. paraded in solemn procession.[41] "Hall's Military Band headed the procession and the Hon. W. C. Philbrook was marshall."[42]

Once the cornerstone was laid, plans were begun for the city centennial to be celebrated the following year. The date was set for Sunday, June 21, 1902, despite the fact that the date for the Colby commencement would have to be changed to avoid a conflict. The new city hall was to be ready for the celebration.

During the autumn months band news was largely overshadowed by the news of Prof. Chapman's Maine Music Festival. Once again Hall had been on tour with Chapman's Maine Symphony Orchestra, and participated as cornetist in the festivals in Portland and Bangor. The *Mail* gave the orchestra a rave review, and said the audiences were ever-larger and more enthusiastic.[43] The remaining months were relatively quiet for Hall and the band, with the usual dances, but not much concert activity.

Program given by Hall's Band for the Colby Commencement, June 1901, as quoted in the Waterville (Maine) Mail, 26 June 1901.

If Hall was out of the news, it might have been that his attention was directed to other matters. Still a bachelor at forty-three, his eye had been caught by a pretty student at Coburn Classical Institute (a college preparatory school in Waterville). Concert publicity took a back seat to courting.

The following winter Hall was married to Izzie (Isabella) Alta Luce, for what has been frequently described as a brief, unhappy marriage. The date, January 29, 1902, is a matter of public record, and as such was one of the few events in Hall's life that previous writers had fastened upon with any certainty. The marriage record shows Hall's age as forty-three, Izzie's as nineteen.

The photo of Mrs. Hall on the next page, was taken two years later, in 1904, when she was twenty-one. Little is known about their courtship. Izzie's mother, Ellen Luce, was a nurse living in Waterville; her father, Prince A. Luce, a physician living on Islesboro, an island in Penobscot Bay. Izzie was said to be popular among the girls at Coburn.

This account of their wedding was given in the *Mail*.

A quiet home wedding took place Wednesday evening at the rooms of Prof. R. B. Hall on Thayer Court. The contracting parties were Miss Izzie A. Luce and Prof. R. B. Hall. Rev. A. A. Lewis of the methodist church officiated and only the relatives and some friends of the parties were present. Prof. Hall's full orchestra furnished music for the occasion. After the ceremony the happy couple took the Pullman for a wedding trip. Mrs. Hall who is the daughter of Mrs. Helen Luce has made a large circle of friends during the three years she has been in this city and at Coburn.

Prof. Hall is one of the best musicians in the state. Coming to this city from Bangor twelve years ago, he has brought the Waterville Military Band to the present high standard and furnished the city with an orchestra to be proud of. He also has a wide reputation as a composer of music, his marches being especially famous. Prof. and Mrs. Hall will be home after Feb. 13.[44]

Of interest is the mention of Hall's rooms on Thayer Court. Prior to this time, his address had been 168 Main St., and his advertisements as a music teacher were also for that address. In the following year's directory (1903) his address was 3 Thayer Court. The wedding story seems to imply that Hall was already residing at Thayer Court at the time of his marriage. It is reasonable to presume that he moved there late in 1901, in anticipation of married life. It must have been a fairly large apartment to accommodate the entire wedding, including a full orchestra of eleven or twelve pieces.

The band had given Hall a bachelor party the previous evening, and according to Varney, it was quite a party. As he told Bardwell in an interview in 1968:

Yeah, all the band men, they fixed up a place in the band room, and they had all these long tables, you know and they had all kinds of eats and— It was a regular blowout, you know, had a good time.[45]

Varney was going out of his way to avoid mentioning the consumption of alcoholic beverages. He also asked Bardwell to stop the tape at this point. He had grown up in a generation of Mainers for whom alcohol was illegal, discussion of alcohol was embarrassing, and the prevailing public attitude was one of teetotalism. When I interviewed Ralph Gould, who had also grown up under prohibition, every time he wanted to mention drinking behavior he would speak in euphemisms for the benefit of the tape recorder while pantomiming "drinking" with his hands and mouth.[46]

PLATE 10. ISABELLA LUCE HALL (Courtesy of Bagaduce Music Lending Library)

Prohibition had been introduced to Maine in 1851 with the nation's first anti-liquor law, known as the "Maine Law." Although it was repealed in 1858, it was eventually written into the state constitution in 1885. Sporadic enforcement, legislative tinkering with the provisions of the saloon law, and local corruption delayed the closing of the saloons throughout the remainder of the 1880's and 1890's, but by the turn of the century Maine was effectively dry, at least as far as saloons and taverns were concerned. Private clubs were another matter,

and many of them flourished during this era. Many of the dances and events for which the band played were occasions for drinking under the auspices of a private club, designed specifically to avoid the saloon law. Consumption of alcohol-based patent medicines and tonics purchased at the pharmacy became commonplace. A barrel of beer was often a feature of the boat excursions on which the band went; on the boat they were beyond the reach of the law. During this era people tried to avoid mentioning consumption of alcohol in polite company, resulting in Varney's euphemism "a regular blowout, you know, had a good time."

Ralph Gould wrote that

R. B. was known to like a drink. There is no recollection, however of his ever appearing in public under the influence. Liquor was a palliative for the man and no doubt offered some respite from his continued physical infirmities.[47]

Other authors have followed the same tactful line. One of Hall's motivations for joining the Canabas Club during this era was that he "could get his beer."[48]

Evidently Hall's bandsmen sensed that he was not happy in his marriage almost from the start. Roundy, who had been studying clarinet with Hall since 1897, and was clarinetist in the band and pianist in the orchestra at the time of Hall's marriage, said of the situation:

Oh Boy! The worst thing he ever did was get married.[49]

His attempt at an explanation fell short of lucidity, and unfortunately Bardwell did not follow up on this aspect of the interview. Roundy seemed to ascribe the trouble to age difference:

* She, he, he didn't, sh, he,he,he,he, was an **old man** when he was married. What I mean, he was uh, He was too old to get married. I don't know.... But he was awful unhappy.[50]

Little news was generated by Hall or the band during the spring of 1902. The summer concerts were assured by the Band's sponsoring corporation, and the frenzy of preparation for the centennial dominated the local news. With his friend and amateur musician, the Honorable ex-mayor Judge Warren C. Philbrook as chairman of the parade committee, and prominent local bank owner Dr. Frederick C. Thayer, a founding member of the Hall's Military Band Corporation, as chief parade marshal, Hall could not have escaped involvement in the musical planning. Hall was placed in charge of the music for the celebration. Judge Philbrook was to be the orator at the ceremony. A five-division parade was planned, with Hall's band leading the first division, the Pittsfield Knights of Pythias band leading the second division, and the Second Regiment band of Lewiston to lead the fifth division.

This lineup of bands was sufficient to assure a spectacular parade, which was given on Tuesday, the third day of the celebration. The remainder of the week-long celebration involved Hall's Band or Orchestra in almost every event. According to the official program for the centennial week, on Sunday evening, June 22, 1902, Hall's Orchestra gave the music at a religious mass meeting to begin the festivities, with several selections between the various speeches and prayers.[51] Monday morning Hall's Orchestra once again played between the speeches at the dedication of the new city hall. The Caecelia Club, which had in earlier times been directed by Judge Philbrook, sang Handel's "Hallelujah Chorus" from the *Messiah*. The *Mail* said the music was "of high order."[52] The keys to the new city hall were presented by the architect, who made a speech.

That same afternoon, Hall's Military Band gave several selections at Monument Park, along with an oration by the Hon. Warren Coffin Philbrook, "lately mayor of Waterville." Monday evening there was a grand illumination of the city, with music by Hall's Orchestra. Tuesday was the grand parade, with Hall's Military Band, "26 men under R. B. Hall, leader," heading the First Division, and other bands in the other divisions as mentioned earlier.[53] On Tuesday evening, the usual concert was given by Hall's Military Band, to an unusually large crowd at Monument Park.

The city was teeming with visitors, and lodgings were in very short supply. Anyone with a spare room rented it to visitors, if out-of-town family had not claimed the space. All the lodges and clubs were offering hospitality to visiting brethren: the *Mail* and the official centennial program booklet carried listings of the addresses of lodges for the convenience of out of town members. Waterville at the time was a city of lodges; there were Elks, Masons, Knights Templar, Odd Fellows, Patriarchs Militant, and the United Order of the Golden Cross. There were Knights of Pythias, Ancient Order of Hibernians, Sons of Veterans, Grand Army of the Republic, American Order of United Workmen, and the Brotherhood of Railway Trainmen. All these had hospitality programs. Amidst all this, the Canabas Club, not a part of a national fraternity, opened its doors to invited guests from corresponding clubs in other cities.

By Thursday evening, activity had shifted to the Colby campus, where Hall's Military Band gave the Promenade Concert to begin the commencement activities. It was at this commencement, according to Gould, that Hall had a stroke and could not pick up his music.[54] That is unlikely, however, because no mention was made in the papers, and Hall was busily performing throughout the summer season of 1902. Additionally, in March of 1905 when Hall had his well documented stroke, it was described as a first stroke, and his prognosis was said to be good because he had not had a stroke before.[55] In any event this was the third successive year that Hall had played the Colby commencement; it was becoming expected of him, whether or not there was a city celebration to compete for his musical services.

In spite of the frenzy of activity surrounding the Centennial, Hall and his orchestra managed to squeeze in a train ride to Hall's boyhood home-town, to play the Richmond school graduation. The *Lewiston Journal,* in writing of the event said:

> *R. B. Hall, leader of this well known musical organization, was formerly of Richmond and first played cornet in the old Richmond Band. His friends at this place have been watching him with interest and showed their admiration for his work by the recognition they gave him. He was encored twice, and the people would not desist with their applause until he favored them with another selection.[56]*

The remainder of 1902 was relatively quiet for Hall. There was lots of orchestra work for dances, and an occasional excursion with the band; the summer concerts were played as usual. The Maine Festival Orchestra performed as usual, though the tour was not as extensive as in some years. Hall's orchestra played regularly in the new city hall auditorium, which was a center for visiting theatrical performances, and needed an orchestra in the pit. The city hall was constructed so that city offices were on the lower levels, with the auditorium, known as the Opera House, occupying the entire floor above them. Although Hall had been participating in pit orchestras and playing solos from the pit ever since his early days with Andrews' Orchestra in the Bangor Opera House, it was here in the Waterville Opera House that, as leader of the orchestra, Hall's music sometimes upstaged the show. Stories of are told of Hall's cornet playing from the pit being encored to the dismay of the actors on stage.

Ralph Gould has provided the best retelling of this story:

> *While leading the theatre orchestra at the opera house in Waterville, Hall came to know many members of the traveling musical companies. They helped spread his fame, for he often stole their show. Instead of applauding the players on the stage, the audience called upon the pit orchestra for encores of its overtures and music between the acts. To the chagrin of the traveling players the show would be held up until the demands of the audience were met. Often, too, one of the orchestra numbers would be a cornet solo, usually written by R. B. Hall.[57]*

Following the pattern established in the previous five years, Hall's publishers brought out just two marches in 1902. They were *The Cavalier*, and *The Crisis*, both published by John Church. Neither of these is among Hall's most widely played today, although both are interesting and well crafted marches.

The Crisis is unique among Hall's works. It is Hall's only march which uses quotes from patriotic airs, and was most likely penned in response to the Spanish American War and the attendant flurry of national fervor it engendered. Short melodic quotes from "Hail Columbia," "Home Sweet Home," and The "Star Spangled Banner," are woven into and interspersed with six-eight strains having a martial and equestrian mood.

The following year little had changed for the band. There was no band news until June, when Hall's Band was listed in the lineup for the Memorial Day parade. The Band went to Portland to play on St. John's Day, June 24, for a large gathering of Knights Templar from all over the state. Since that conflicted with Colby College's commencement, the college hired the Belfast Band to furnish music.

Breaking with the publishing pattern of the previous six years, Hall changed publishers in search of a better royalty arrangement, and brought forth only one march; but that one was a huge success. The year 1903 provided Hall's greatest financial triumph in the form of *Officer of the Day,* one of his most famous and widely sold marches. A six-eight march, in the popular two-step style that had been all the rage since John Philip Sousa's *Washington Post* came out in 1890, *Officer of the Day* had an interesting story concerning its origin. According to Arthur Roundy, who was there at the time, Hall had taken a funeral march, or dirge, that he had previously written, and converted it to six-eight. The manuscript band parts were laid out on tables in the band hall, and Roundy helped Hall to paste together the parts for the new march.[59]

That transformation may be hard to imagine except for the trio,[61] but in any event, as soon as the piece was published it became a popular hit. Lyon and Healy published it for piano, band, and orchestra, and Hall collected royalties on it.

The Crisis March, by R. B. Hall. Solo Cornet part.[58]

According to Varney, as quoted in Bridges, the royalties were only two cents a copy for piano sheets, but three hundred thousand piano copies were sold in a single shipment to Europe, not to mention his American sales, and the piece was a huge financial success for Hall.[62] By my figuring that one shipment would have produced a royalty check of $6,000.00, a very considerable sum at that time! Gould, Varney, and others relate that when the royalty check came, Hall took the entire check to the Canabas Club, and his wife didn't see him for some time. It is possible that this sum was at least in part Hall's entry dues to the club, or perhaps a repayment for dues money that had been loaned to him by Philbrook or Webb, or another of his sponsors.

The Canabas Club was a posh gathering place for the élite businessmen of Waterville. There were three floors of beautifully furnished lounges and meeting rooms, a fine piano, a billiards room, and a ballroom for functions. Since prohibition had closed the saloons, it was one of the few places where a man could get a beer, or keep a locker with a bottle in it. The membership list of about sixty included W. C. Philbrook, and most of the businessmen who formed Hall's Military Band Corporation. The Canabas club was said to be one of Hall's favorite haunts. He had played dances there ever since his early days with Dinsmore's Orchestra, but in those early days he never could have expected to become a member.

Hall's march *Canabas* was published by Lyon and Healy the following year (1904), and the piano version became very popular at dancing classes and social dances. Lyon and Healy sent Hall a new cornet, which he did not like, and did not play, preferring his familiar Boston Three Star.[63]

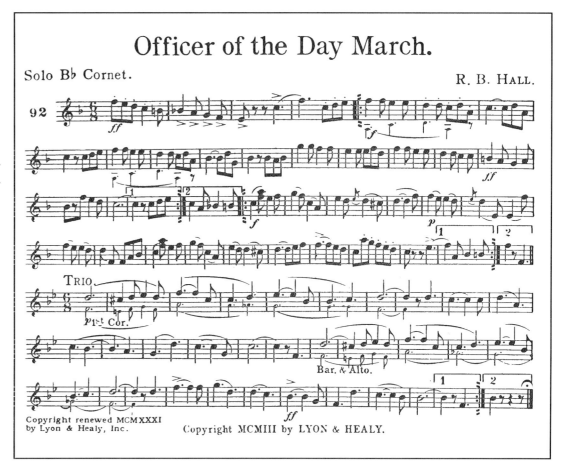

Officer of the Day March, by R. B. Hall. Solo Cornet part.[60]

In addition to *Canabas*, two other Hall marches were published in 1904: *Glenwood*, adding to Hall's publications by John Church; and *Trinity Bells*, the third of his marches published by Lyon and Healy. *Trinity Bells*, which had been written several years earlier, was dedicated to Hall's sister Alice (Mrs. Nelson Thurlow) a church organist in Richmond. With all this publishing activity, and the popularity of Hall's marches, Mace

Gay brought out a collection of sixteen of the marches he had published for Hall during the 1890's. Entitled *Mace Gay's Book of Hall's Marches,* it was the first all-Hall collection to be published. Because Hall had sold his marches outright to Mace Gay, he did not receive any royalties from this collection; however, their popularity increased the market for his more recent marches, for which he did have royalty arrangements.

H all's orchestra was busy all that winter playing dances in a series organized by "eight young belles of the city."[64] These dances were held at the Armory, which was only one of several good venues for dancing in Waterville at the time.

The Waterville Military Band was very active and doing well with dances all winter, and in June announced their new uniforms.

NEW UNIFORMS RECEIVED

Twenty new Waterville Military Band uniforms arrived Friday from Philadelphia Made To Measure. The uniforms are of fine black cloth elaborately braided. The trimmings are of silver instead of the more usual gold. The caps have a silver W.M.B. monogram.

PLATE 11. WATERVILLE MILITARY BAND In Their New Uniforms (Courtesy of Bagaduce Music Lending Library)

Without a doubt these are the finest band uniforms in the state, and the boys made their initial appearance in them last Sunday at Lakewood in Skowhegan. The money for the new suits was earned by giving social dances the past winter at the Mesalonskee Pavilion, and owing to the popularity of these events the band will continue holding them, giving one each month.[65]

It is of interest that the Band was affluent enough to purchase new uniforms on the basis of dances for which it was the sponsor. Also noteworthy is the fact that the uniforms were monogrammed for the Waterville Military Band rather than Hall's Military Band, as they were just as often known at that time. An example of this dual naming is found in the notice of an extra concert in addition to the usual summer series (which was by now so predictable that it seldom received press notice). "The Band concert given by Hall's Military Band on the lawn of the Universalist Church Wednesday Evening was enjoyed by a large gathering of people."[66] Years later when Bardwell tried to establish just which name the band had been known by, both Roundy and Varney were adamant (even if erroneously so) that it was known as "Hall's Band" until after his death.[67]

The following year (1905) was marked by Hall's involvement with the Elks lodge in Waterville. Hall's Orchestra began the year with a "Senior Hop" at the Elks hall with 50 couples attending.[68] The Elks were expanding, and a new lodge was under construction at the time.

Club and lodge involvement was perhaps at its peak during these years in Waterville. The *Mail* regularly announced their events, and the lodges themselves took advertisements to announce their regular meetings and functions. The lodges all went by their initials, a fact that made any announcement read like alphabet soup. The clubs, for the most part, had names, albeit cryptic ones. In a two-week period during 1905 meetings were held for: Waterville Lodge #371 I.O.G.T. (International Order of Good Templars); Waterville Lodge #33 F.&A.M. (Free and Accepted Masons); Canton Halifax Patriarchs Militant, I.O.O.F.; Samaritan Lodge #39 I.O.O.F. (Independent Order of Odd Fellows); G.A.R. (Grand Army of the Republic); Garfield Camp S.V. (Sons of Veterans); Martha Washington Chapter O.E.S. (Order of the Eastern Star); Kennebec Pomona Grange; Waterville Lodge No. 5, A.O.U.W. (American Order of United Workmen); Waterville Lodge #231, N.E.O.P. (New England Order of Protection); and Havelock Lodge #35, K. of P. (Knights of Phythias).

Clubs included: The F.H. Club (no explanation); Ho Mita Koda (Hawaiian for "Welcome my friend"); Merry Peppers (young ladies temperance refreshments social club); and Nonesuch (a whist club).[69]

A similar period in March and April included activities of most of the foregoing groups plus the formation of a Utopian club, and regular meetings of: Canabas Club; V-2 Eyes Club; Saint Omer Commandery K.T. (Knights Templar); United Order of the Golden Cross; Hamilton Lodge Degree of Honor; Knights of Columbus; F.B.(no explanation); and Kennebec Lodge #234 Brotherhood of Railway Train Men.[70] The neighboring communities of Oakland, Fairfield and Vassalboro all had similarly active club and lodge announcements.

What was not announced was that many of these clubs flourished because they provided a strategem for avoiding the ever-stricter enforcement of the saloon laws. Other clubs announced their temperance stance to provide a social opportunity for the "dry minded."

Not only were clubs and lodges popular and important, but there were many bands being formed and performing in the area as well. The Mechanics Band of Oakland, Waterville's Lockwood Mills Band and Boutelle's (French) Band, as well as local amateur bands in Fairfield and other nearby towns all received occasional notice.

A new band was being formed in Newport, and Hall had been engaged to teach it. He rode the train up on Fridays, taught in the afternoon and rehearsed in the evening, returning on Saturday. According to the *Mail*: "The Professor is a good teacher and the band ought to be a good one."[71]

When the new Elks Lodge was opened at the end of February, Hall once again was called upon for a concert and ball. "Dancing to a late hour" was a favored pastime, and followed most of the meetings and installations of officers.[72] That ball on February 27, 1905, may well have been Hall's last appearance before the night of his stroke.

Hall's march *Exalted Ruler* is dedicated to the Waterville Elks Lodge, and was published by John Church in 1905. This march, and his involvement at Elks functions, produced a strong enough association that one of Hall's obituaries stated that he was an Elks member, although all other information contradicts that. A grand convention was scheduled in the new Elks Lodge, with visiting dignitaries from other cities in Maine for the first week in March.[73] That would have made the weekend dates March 4 and 5. Probably Hall's new march, which had alternating six-eight and two-four sections in what was then the newest quadrille style, was intended to be introduced that Saturday evening.

In any event *Exalted Ruler* (which is usually given the sobriquet of "Hall's last march") was newly completed when Hall went to rehearsal on March 2nd. According to the *Waterville Sentinel*, the new march that was to be dedicated to the Elks Lodge was "completed but a day or two" before Hall was taken ill.[75]

The *Mail's* account of the evening follows:

SUFFERS A SHOCK

The Exalted Ruler March by R. B. Hall. Solo Cornet part.[74]

Prof. R. B. Hall Stricken With Paralysis While Conducting a Band Rehearsal Thursday Night.

Professor R. B. Hall, the well known band master and local March King, lies in a critical condition today as the result of a shock with which he was stricken while conducting a rehearsal at the band rooms Thursday evening.

Prof. Hall was enjoying his usual good health Thursday, and was joking with the band boys before the rehearsal. The rehearsal had been in progress only a few moments when the members noticed that Mr. Hall's expression quickly changed, and he sank back in his chair. Eugene Dearborn rushed to him and found that he was apparently dead. Medical aid was summoned and Dr. Abbott arrived very quickly and pronounced it a paralytic shock. Dr. Abbott advised taking Mr. Hall to his home at once, which was done, and Dr. L. G. Bunker, the family physician, was immediately summoned. The doctors worked over him and after a considerable time he showed signs of reviving but was still unconscious. It was found that the shock had affected the right side of the body.

Dr. Bunker has been in attendance today and he reports the patient as getting along as well as could be expected, and he thinks that as this is the first shock there is no doubt but that he will recover in time the full use of the affected parts, although perhaps it will be a slow process.

Prof. Hall's many friends in the city learned of his great misfortune with the deepest regret and concern and all will hope earnestly for his full recovery.[76]

Elsewhere in the same paper, in the local news column, a brief report appeared, indicating a substantial improvement in Hall's condition.

The condition of Prof. R. B. Hall was much improved Monday, even beyond the expectation of his attending physician. He is gaining wonderfully and every day marks a great change for the better in his condition.[77]

One of the peculiarities of examining a particular century-old event from the vantage of a weekly newspaper is the effect it has of telescoping events into a weekly summary. Just as a view through a telephoto lens tends to flatten the perspective of the object seen, so the weekly summary condenses fast moving events in a way that minimizes the suspense that must have been felt at the moment. Thus the weekly *Waterville Mail*, which was published on Wednesdays during this era, carried all the news from Thursday, March 2, to Wednesday, March 8, in a single issue. A smaller Friday supplement was being published and distributed at this time, but was not saved or microfilmed. Important stories were usually carried again the following Wednesday. The story of Hall's stroke had run in the Friday edition, March 3, 1905, but was also run in the larger Wednesday edition. The Wednesday *Mail* was still the paper of record for Waterville in

this era; although the *Sentinel*, newly a daily, was soon to assume that role. So it is in the same issue of the *Mail*, that the Elks convention, Hall's stroke, and the follow up story indicating Hall's recovery, are all reported.

Hall improved rapidly that spring, and was soon back on his feet. Although later writers were to remark that this was "an illness from which he never fully recovered" and in retrospect that is quite true, Dr. Bunker's sanguine prognosis (reported in the news story) seemed at the time to be correct. Three weeks after the initial report, the *Mail* was able to say:

The many friends of Prof. R. B. Hall will be pleased to know that he has so far recovered as to be able to walk down town Wednesday afternoon. The Professor is gaining rapidly now, and hopes in a short time to be able to lead his musical organizations.[78]

Also reported in the same issue was a testimonial to Hall, which was well attended and "highly successful" in raising some funds to help the Professor in his crisis. The following month Hall was indeed back to leading his musical organizations. On Wednesday, April 26, the *Mail* reported:

Prof. R. B. Hall was able to direct his band Tuesday for the first time since he was stricken with a shock several weeks ago. The band boys were right glad to see him back in his old position and the music loving people of Waterville are glad that the Professor will be able to direct the band concerts this summer.[79]

The *Sentinel* also ran local news, and on April 5, reported that Prof. Hall was "gaining steadily" and that he would "soon be enjoying about his usual health."[80]

A week later the band was ready to give a dance, and the *Sentinel* reported that:

There will be a dance given in the armory on May 11 by Hall's Military Band. The music for the dance will be played by the full band and a large crowd will undoubtedly be in attendance.[81]

The Waterville Military Band was back in action, and Hall's busy life as a conductor, teacher, and orchestra director was continuing without abatement. Memorial Day, Hall led the band in morning Memorial exercises, the afternoon parade, and the evening concert program.[82]

Later that summer, Hall must have been gratified at the attention paid to his former student F. Louise Horne when she was honored for attaining the position of soloist in a Boston orchestra.[83] Louise Horne had moved from Cambridge, Maine, to Waterville as a teenager to study cornet with Hall between 1892 and 1896. It was she who had filled in as solo cornet when Hall was away during 1895. She later became renowned as a female cornet virtuoso and toured extensively, living in Waterville between engagements. A model for other young women, she led the V-2 Eyes Club (a social club for career-minded young women) whose meetings she hosted at her home on Pleasant Street in Waterville.[84] She was married in 1910 in Kansas, and gave up touring, though she continued to teach there.[85]

NOTES

[1] Ralph Gould, "R. B. Hall - Maine's Music Man," *Down East*, October 1967, 33.

[2] *Turner's Augusta, Hallowell, Gardiner and Waterville Directory*, (Auburn, Maine: A. R. Turner Publishing Co., 1897), 499.

[3] *Waterville* [Maine] *Morning Sentinel*, 28 May 1977, 9.

[4] Gould, op.cit.

[5] Rehrig, *The Heritage Encyclopedia of Band Music*, 312.

[6] *Waterville* [Maine] *Mail*, 7 June 1899, 4. (Hereafter, *WM*).

[7] *WM*, 7 June 1899, 5.

[8] *WM*, 21 June 1899, 3.

[9] *WM*, 12 July 1899, 4.

[10] Varney, NA#2228.045.

[11] Edwards, *Music and Musicians of Maine*, 350.

[12] *WM*, 14 June 1899.

[13] *WM*, 12 July 1899, 5.

[14] Gould, *Down East*, 31.

[15] Fossett, *LJ*, 22 March 1952.

[16] Varney, NA#2228.054-55.

[17] *WM*, 2 August 1899, 1.

[18] Ibid.

[19] *WM*, 2 August 1899.

[20] *WM*, 9 August 1899.

[21] *WM*, 23 August 1899.

[22] *LJ*, 7 Sepetmber 1899.

[23] *WM*, 13 September 1899.

[24] *WM*, 18 October 1899.

[25] Ibid.

[26] *WM*, 3 January 1900.

[27] *WM*, 17 January 1900.

[28] Edwin Carey Whittemore, *The Centennial History of Waterville*, (Waterville, Maine: Executive Committee of the Centennial, 1902), 409.

[29] *WM*, 23 May 1900.

[30] *WM*, 26 June 1900.

[31] *WM*, 29 August 1900, 6.

[32] Ibid.

[33] *WM*, 14 November 1900.

[34] *WM*, 17 April, 24 April, 15 May 1901.

[35] *WM*, 14 April 1901.

[36] *WM*, 29 May 1901.

[37] *WM*, Ibid.

[38] *WM*, 26 June 1901.

[39] *WM*, Ibid.

[40] *WM*, Ibid.

[41] Abbreviations for the Masonic orders were used extensively in the news and in advertising. In this case K. T. is for Knights Templars, and F. & A. M. stands for Free and Accepted Masons, the basic Masonic order.

[42] *WM*, 21 August 1901, 6.

[43] *WM*, 9 October 1901.

[44] *WM*, 5 February 1902, 6.

[45] NA#2261.056-57.

[46] NA#2262.

[47] Gould, *Down East*, 32-33.

[48] Bridges, *Pioneers in Brass*, 45.

[49] NA#2261.038.

[50] Ibid.

[51] *1802-1902 Waterville Centennial Official Program*, (Waterville, Maine: no ed. or pub., 1902).

[52] *WM*, 25 June 1902.

[53] Ibid.

NOTES, CONT.

[54] Gould, *Down East*, 33.

[55] *WM*, 8 March 1905.

[56] *LJ*, 15 June 1902, reprinted in *WM*, 18 June 1902.

[57] Gould, *Down East*, 31-32.

[58] R. B. Hall, *The Crisis*, (Cincinnati, Ohio: John Church, 1902).

[59] NA#2228.008.

[60] R. B. Hall, *Officer of the Day*, (Chicago, Illinois: Lyon & Healey, 1903).

[61] Perhaps the pasting part was the assembly of the "converted" trio with existing or newly written six-eight first and second strains, which would make sense.

[62] Bridges, *Pioneers in Brass*, 45.

[63] Roundy, NA#2228.011.

[64] *WM*, 6 January 1904.

[65] *WM*, 15 June 1904, 5.

[66] *WM*, 20 July 1904, 6.

[67] NA#2261.022.

[68] *WM*, 4 January 1905.

[69] WM, 25 January, 1 February 1905.

[70] WM, 15 February, 8 March 1905.

[71] *WM*, 4 January 1905, 6.

[72] *WM*, 1 February, 8 February, 15 February 1905.

[73] *WM*, 8 March 1905.

[74] R. B. Hall, *Exalted Ruler*, (Cincinnati, Ohio: John Church, 1905).

[75] *WS*, 13 June 1905.

[76] *WM*, 8 March 1905, 6.

[77] Ibid., 4.

[78] *WM*, 29 March 1905, 6.

[79] *WM*, 26 April 1905, 6.

[80] *WS*, 5 April 1905, 4.

[81] *WS*, 9 May 1905, 4.

[82] *WS*, 27 May 1905.

[83] *WM*, 21 July 1905, 6.

[84] *WM*, 12 April 1905, 5.

[85] Bridges, *Pioneers in Brass*, 48b.

CHAPTER NINE
HALL'S FINAL YEARS (1905-1907)

Following the triple Memorial Day appearances, the summer of 1905 continued busier than ever for Hall. There was the Oak Grove[1] commencement on June 7, for which Hall's Orchestra played.[2] The monthly dance at the Armory was given by the full Waterville Military Band the following evening, Thursday, June 8. It had become a regular event ever since the drive to buy new uniforms began. According to the *Sentinel*: "A good crowd was present, and as the music for the dances was played by the full band, it was no small part of the entertainment."[3] The very next day Hall went to Newport to teach the Friday evening band class, something he had begun just before his stroke.

Professor R. B. Hall went to Newport yesterday afternoon, where he gave instruction to the Newport band at the rehearsal in the evening.[4]

The following week, he took not just one, but two orchestras to Orono to play at the University of Maine commencement, intending to be gone the remainder of the week.[5] He returned to news of a contract for the entire two days of music at the opening of the Central Maine State Fair's new building, housing an exhibition hall, auditorium, and skating rink. The remainder of the month was filled with band concerts at the new coliseum (skating rink) and an excursion to Lakewood,

with a big crowd expected to accompany the band on the train.

In mid-June, the *Sentinel* ran a lengthy and laudatory career retrospective on Hall which they had lifted from the *Portland Sunday Times*. This was the peak of Hall's popularity, and the story cited examples of his music being played around the world, as well as at home. It lauded his legendary cornet tone and execution, which had brought him so much attention as a cornet soloist. It mentioned many of his marches by name, and praised his output in quantity and quality. This feature story was later to become the model for Hall's obituaries, most of which incorporated it in its entirety.[6] The photo of Hall on this page was taken at about this time.

His recent incapacitation notwithstanding, Hall's schedule did not seem to be that of an invalid. To the contrary, he seemed busier and more active than ever in the summer of 1905, both with the band and with his orchestra.

The summer concert series could not begin until July 20 that year, because the bandstand provided by the city was not ready, but as soon as it was put into place Hall started the concerts.[7] The following week the concert was followed immediately by a dance at Mesalonskee Hall, another popular dance venue in Waterville; music for dancing was played by the full band.[8]

The summer concert series went ahead at this very busy pace, with Hall, in spite of his partial paralysis, directing the band before large crowds and garnering the usual favorable reviews. The concerts continued well into September. Absent were the cornet solos which had been a feature of Hall's concerts in previous seasons. They were replaced by baritone solos, *In the Moonlight*, which had been published in 1893, and *Geraldine Caprice* which was published in 1906. These solos could have been cornet solos, and as a matter of fact, the published parts for *Geraldine* call it a "cornet capriccio." They

were very melodious and less virtuosic in character than a Hall cornet solo, and therefore appropriate both technically and musically for the baritone horn.

Hall's tone on the cornet had been legendary. Although he was never again to regain his full power or facility on the instrument, the memory of that tone lingered in the minds of his pupils and bandsmen as the special quality in his playing. Although his execution was always said to be faultless, it was beauty and "perfect finish" of his tone that set his playing apart. The *Sentinel* described his sound thus:

When executing difficult performances on the cornet it is impossible to mistake the full, round, rich, luscious singing tone which emanates from the instrument. He plays with telling expression and perfect finish of tone production.[9]

Sixty-three years later, Arthur Roundy was to describe the sound of Hall's cornet playing as if he still heard it perfectly in his mind.

You know R. B. Hall got the most beautiful tone on a cornet of any person I ever heard blow a horn in my life. And one day I said to him—I was a kid asking questions—"Mr. Hall, how did you learn to get such a beautiful tone?" "Why," he says, "I never fool. Every time I play my

PLATE 12. R. B. HALL, AGE 45 (Courtesy of Bagaduce Music Lending Library)

cornet, I try to make it sound better than it ever did before. Every time it must sound better." And I believe if he was in another room playing right now, you'd think it was a lady with a fine voice humming. You would never connect it with a brass instrument.[10]

Through the remainder of 1905 Hall continued to direct the band, though he was unable at first to play the cornet. Gradually, working along with his pupil James Varney, who was just beginning, Hall regained the ability to play, though not with his former power. Varney, who was Hall's last cornet pupil, told of Hall trying to demonstrate triple tonguing at a lesson: by inspiring his student he inspired himself to relearn.

*Ayuh. Well, I'll tell you: When I first started in, he was teaching me to triple tongue. And of course he'd been paralyzed and he wasn't able to play at all. But he took a notion, along in the fall, to-uh, just to egg me on, you know. He was going to race with me. 'Course I was just starting in, and so he really did it, and he used to compete with me, you know, just a little bit, on my lessons. And after he got so he found that he could blow a little bit, and he went out to-uh. He got a job for his old, they wanted 'Hall's Orchestra,' for a New Year's ball over to Winthrop.[11]

Hall's orchestra had been playing very busily throughout the summer, with engagements at graduations and lodge dances. Varney's testimony indicates that Hall did not personally play the cornet at these, since his lip had not yet returned, but merely provided the orchestra and perhaps conducted. The New Year's ball at Kent's Hill Academy in Winthrop was different, though. He actually went to play his cornet. This must have distressed or offended his wife: one can only guess at what the daughter of a nurse would think of a man going out to play all night after such a long and precarious recuperation. Varney's tale continues:

*And so he went. He'd got so he could play a little bit, and he decided he would go and play the job. But when he got home from Winthrop, (He had some beautiful paintings, and nice silverware that his mother had given him at the time of their marriage, and things like that) she flew the coop and took everything with her.[12]

Gould had phrased it more succinctly: "While he was playing at a New Year's Ball in Winthrop, Maine, Mrs. Hall packed up her things at home and left her husband."[13]

Most unfortunately, the *Mail* for January 3, 1906 is missing from the collection (January 4, 1904 was microfilmed in its place) so no local news account of this domestic tragedy is available. The *Mail* for January 10 reports Hall's Orchestra at a Knights of Pythias dance, but that is the last time it is mentioned.

Varney is also the source for the other significant anecdote from this era in Hall's life, concerning the only recording that Hall ever made. It was unfortunately broken in an incident which happened in Varney's presence. In a letter to Glen Bridges, Varney wrote:

*...his own version of the carnival of Venice. He had made a record of this on the old type Cylinder records. As I was studying his arrangement, he wanted to play it for me, which he did. He was crippled considerably and as he removed the record from the machine he dropped it, and it smashed on the floor. We felt badly and his wife cried, the only time I ever saw any display of emotion from her.[14]

Years later, telling the same tale he emphasized the beauty of the arrangement.

*I was at his house the day he broke it, he. It was his arrangement of "Carnival of Venice" and it was beautiful. But he was clumsy after he'd had this shock, you know. And it was one of those cylinder, old wax cylinder records they used to have on the Edison machine. And he went to push that off, and it went into the floor. And it was his own arrangement of "Carnival of Venice," yes, and it was beautiful.[15]

As few as they are, the available descriptions of Hall's apartment and furnishings seem to indicate that he was by then living in considerable comfort for the time. An Edison phonograph was a luxury item found in very few homes in 1905. The Thayer court apartment must have been spacious to accommodate his wedding, together with a twelve-piece orchestra, and the paintings and silver that Isabella is said to have taken when she left were the accoutrements of a comfortable life. Although Hall had received little money for his earlier marches, having sold some of them outright, later publishers such as Church and Fischer did provide royalties for march composers. Lyon and Healy offered the most liberal royalties in the business at the time, which is probably why Hall switched publishers in 1903. Hall's life at the time, and the life Isabella left, was not one of poverty.

The following year, as Hall's health deteriorated, he moved to Portland to stay with his mother and sister at their home at 59 High Street. This would have been in the late winter of 1907. Varney was supposed to go down to visit during the summer and study with him, but that never came to pass. The Waterville Military Band and Hall's Orchestra were turned over to the leadership of cornetist Robert L. Wentworth, who had been a pupil of Hall's. Hall's Orchestra was now known as Wentworth's Orchestra.[16]

Hall died at his mother's home on June 8, 1907. The official cause of death appeared on the death certificate as: "Uraemia leh. Inv. nephritis." In common terms this was described in the newspapers as Bright's disease; for the non-medical person, that is "kidney failure." He was aged 48 years, eleven months.

All the major Maine newspapers ran lengthy obituaries, mostly based on the June, 1905, career retrospective that had been run in the *Portland Sunday Times,* and then repeated in the *Waterville Sentinel.*[17] The *Bangor News* followed the obituary with a repeat of a humorous story written by a close friend of Hall's, the blind newspaper humorist J. M. Crone. His gentle leg-pulling is written from the perspective of a non-musical person attending a band rehearsal of Hall's *Trinity Bells,* and comparing it to mill noises.[18]

Hall's Waterville Sentinel obituary was slightly different from all the others. It was not based on the *Portland Sunday Times* piece, but made more of Hall's prominence as a citizen of Waterville. It favored R. B. Hall's contributions to Waterville's musi-

PLATE 13. R. B. HALL'S GRAVE-STONE (Courtesy of Raymond Fogler Library Special Collections)

cal scene as well as mentioning many of his compositions. It stated that Hall was a member of the Elks as well as the Canabas Club.

Hall's *Richmond Bee* obituary, no longer available in print (since the *Richmond Bee* offices were closed and the back files removed from the library) was read into a tape recorder by Bardwell in 1967.[19] Though based on the same 1905 retrospective, it is slightly different in emphasis. As befits a family home-town obituary, it stresses Hall's gentle and musical nature, and closes with a poem.

A small delegation from the Waterville Military Band came to the Evergreen Cemetery in Richmond for Hall's interment, and played *Marche Funebre* on the way in to the gravesite and *Independentia* on the way out. Sometime later a relatively large granite memorial was placed at the grave. It bears a large monogram "H" flanked by boughs, and a depiction of Hall's cornet engraved in the granite. The inscription is simply "Robert B. Hall, 1858-1907"; there is no epitaph. On the obverse of the stone are listed the dates of Hall's mother, father, and sisters.

The lack of an epitaph on the granite stone is redressed in print in several places. Fleming in *Richmond on the Kennebec* concluded: "Robert Hall had given to the world melody, rhythm, beautiful music, and a life of kindliness and courtesy."[20] Luther C. Bateman, closed his 1922 feature on Hall with an epitaph:

The very soul of Bert Hall was touched by the spell of music. Such a genius comes only at rare intervals. For Him:

There was music in the sighing of a reed,

There was music in the gushing of a rill:

There was music in all things that reached his ears,

His earth was but an echo of the spheres.[21]

Leaving considerations of poetry aside, Bateman was inspired by the genuine affection held for Hall by the people of Richmond, whom he interviewed, even fifteen years after Hall's death.

CONCLUDING THOUGHTS ABOUT HALL'S LIFE STORY.

After considering the details of R. B. Hall's life and career, the question remains: what was it that made Hall's life different from that of many other musicians of his day? Why is he so uniquely remembered? The answer is really in two parts: first, Hall was not only a bandsman, teacher and leader, but also a cornet soloist widely acclaimed in his day, as well as an orchestral and dance musician. Secondly, Hall composed many well constructed and pleasing marches that were playable by bands of the type he taught, and therefore playable by similar small town bands the world over.

Hall's fame as a soloist and performer was ephemeral, lasting only as long as he kept on performing. As a teacher, his influence lasted a generation among the musicians he taught and the bands he led. In these aspects R. B. Hall was not all that different from many regionally acclaimed musicians of his day. But it was through the marches he composed that his legacy endured the longest, and his influence spread the farthest.

Gould, Roundy, and Varney all attributed the comparative lack of recognition from which Hall's career suffered to the basic fact that he was from Maine. Maine men all, they were giving vent to an ingrained prejudice that so many Maine people manifest, that the local product can never be competitive on an equal footing with that from other, more populous, places. Bardwell's opinion, that Hall's lack of wide recognition stemmed from the fact that he did not engage an impresario to promote constant national and world touring, as Sousa and Gilmore did, is probably closer to the truth. Touring virtuosi were plentiful in Hall's day, and although his tone was reputedly magnificent and his execution flawless, his constant difficulties with his health made the life of a touring artist impractical for him, and that of a world-traveling bandmaster even less so.

Ultimately Hall's compositions carried his fame. They became famous throughout the U. S. and in England and Europe by their merit. Their accessibility to smaller bands, more like the bands that Hall taught and directed, has made them beloved of bandsmen even if audiences today are quicker to recognize a march by Sousa.

During his lifetime Hall moved from place to place in Maine, and even made a few forays out of the state in an effort to earn a better livelihood as a musician. Each move was predicated upon the prospects for a better paying dance orchestra to play in, or a better supported band to lead. In this he was hampered by lifelong physical difficulties, including lameness, and respiratory difficulties that manifested themselves in periods of stress. These infirmities tended to cause him to seek a career in a familiar environment, and not to migrate permanently to a large city in search of wider exposure.

His lameness was worst during his early years and teens, when stories tell of him needing a crutch and being in pain. It seemed to be less of a problem during his twenties and early thirties, when stories tell of him leading the parade with his cane over his arm, or merely walking with a limp. It manifested itself somewhat more strongly in his later years, after age thirty-five, when he abandoned his Albany job because of the heavy requirement for marching. No source has determined whether this condition resulted from a birth defect, an imperfectly healed accident or injury, or a disease such as polio, but whichever was the case it had a profound influence on his career.

His respiratory difficulties, though called consumption by some informants, may or may not have actually been tuberculosis. It is true that there was an epidemic of tuberculosis during the 1880's, especially in the cities. It is also possible that R. B. Hall may have had a lesser condition such as a persistent cold weather catarrh, a sinus infection, bronchitis or similar illness that was exacerbated by continued practice on the cornet. Whatever the case in this respect, Hall's health seemed better in Bangor and Waterville than when he tried his luck in Portland, Philadelphia, Albany, or Springfield. Each of these episodes culminated in his speedy return to Waterville to recuperate.

Hall was thus looking for an opportunity to make his career in a place in which he could stay healthy, or as healthy as possible. His criteria appeared to be: less marching, plenty of fresh air and sunlight, and a good band with a steady income. He found Waterville to be most favorable for his purposes, although garnering a steady income was definitely a problem until after the formation of the Hall's Band Corporation and the eventual granting of royalties by some march publishers. There, he could perform and teach in order to make a living. The Waterville Military Band gave him the opportunity to rehearse and perfect his compositions, and the long winters gave him time to compose the marches that eventually brought him enduring fame.

During his lifetime Hall conducted many different bands. There were two major bands of which he held leadership for a lengthy period of time: the Waterville Military Band (fifteen years) and the Bangor Band (about eight years.) There were two major bands which he led for a shorter time, the American Cadet Band, and the Tenth Regiment Band, each about six months. There was, of course, the Richmond (Cornet) Band which formed the springboard and training ground for his career for six youthful years, off and on. Then there were numerous other Maine bands which he was engaged to teach, for shorter periods of time, in Winterport, Dexter, Cherryfield, Garland, Newport, just to name a few. For these he was the teacher, but not identified so closely as the leader.

Of these bands, only the Bangor Band has survived uninterruptedly to the present. The Waterville Military Band was reorganized at the time of Hall's death, and defunct within twenty years. The American Cadet Band was reabsorbed into Chandler's Band after a few years. The Tenth Regiment Band eventually was remilitarized and followed the battalion to New York City, where it lasted until the National Guard reorganized the Tenth out of existence. The Cherryfield band remained under the leadership of the Wakefield family, first Percy Wakefield, then his son Charlie, and proudly carried the tradition of Hall's marches until 1956, when it disbanded. The Richmond band ceased to exist shortly after 1900, and the various attempts to revive it were all short lived. Newport, Garland, and the other small town cornet bands for which Hall was teacher for a season or two were all blessed with the characteristic impermanence of such undertakings. Although each of these bands was highly regarded (at least locally) while under Hall's tutelage and leadership, Hall's cachet did not assure a band of continuing success.

In some of these communities bands have been restarted in recent years. In Waterville, the R. B. Hall Memorial Band, formed in 1956, is probably the most firmly established of these. The public school bands in Newport have achieved notable success, but they belong to the public school tradition, a different tradition from the town bands that Hall coached there ninety years ago. It may be fairly said that these bands do not represent a continuous organizational heritage with the bands that Hall led.

It was not Hall's personal or musical influence that equipped the surviving bands for their longevity, but rather the strength of the organization supporting the bands that enabled them to hire Hall during the years he was their leader. The single one of Hall's bands that has survived continuously to the present, the Bangor Band, is the one that was incorporated before its time with Hall, and has remained a corporate entity ever since, independently of whomever was leader.

During his years in Bangor and Waterville, Hall had many students, some of whom, like Louise Horne, had careers as famed performers, others of whom, like Arthur Roundy or Wm. D. Haines, were respected music educators and composers in their own right. Still others, like James Varney, were lifelong professional band musicians, or like Dr. Fred Maxfield, were dedicated avocational players. Like the bands, however, as time went on each of these students eventually stopped playing, and the students of the students, though they may carry some of the knowledge handed down from Hall, would have had no actual contact with Hall's charisma.

Hall's legacy to the world, then, was not his bands themselves, nor his students, but his music. At his death his personal music making was at an end, but his marches continue to be played by bands even up to the present. The progress of his music continued after his death with publication of the manuscripts he had completed, followed by publication of many pieces from a collection of his discarded strains, work in progress, and juvenilia. Hall's published marches keep his name before the public even now, nearly a century after his death.

NOTES

[1] Oak Grove was a girls' boarding school located a few miles south of town on the Winslow side of the river.

[2] *Waterville* [Maine] *Sentinel*, 8 July 1905. (Hereafter *WS*).

[3] WS, 9 June 1905.

[4] *WS*, 10 June 1905.

[5] *WS*, 14 June 1905.

[6] *WS*, 13 June 1905.

[7] *WS*, 20 July 1905.

[8] *WS*, 25 July 1905.

[9] *WS*, 13 June 1905.

[10] NA#2261.022-023.

[11] NA#2261.047-48.

[12] NA#2261.048.

[13] Gould, *Down East*, 33.

[14] Varney, quoted in Bridges, *Pioneers in Brass*, 45.

[15] NA#2261.050.

[16] *WS*, 10 June 1907.

[17] *WS*, 13 June 1905.

[18] *Bangor* [Maine] *News*, 10 June 1907, 10.

[19] The original of this tape is among the items in the Bardwell Collection at Fogler Library, University of Maine, Orono Maine. It has not been transcribed or archived in NAFOH. I have a cassette copy of the original for reference.

[20] Fleming, *Richmond on the Kennebec*, 132.

[21] L. C. Bateman, *LJ*, 17 July 1922.

CHAPTER TEN
THE POSTHUMOUS MARCHES

At the time of his death Hall had published 60 marches, and 8 other pieces for band, including his solos and schottisches, through arrangements with various publishers. He had written numerous other marches and pieces that were played by his bands and orchestras, but these were in manuscript. His music was being played by bands all over the country, and his pieces were all selling very well, although only a few of them produced royalties.

His wife, although she had left him at the time of the New Year's dance incident, was nevertheless his widow, and as such she inherited all his effects. Among these was a barrel full of manuscript that contained strains of the various pieces Hall was working on, but that for one reason or another he had rejected, not completed, or set aside for later. Isabella arranged, over the next several years, to have these loose strains assembled into marches and published, and to have the unpublished scores of various marches (and a few other pieces) put in print. These were later to become known as the "rain barrel" marches, since they were literally left in a "rain barrel."

Some of them were reasonably complete as manuscript scores, perhaps for orchestra rather than band. An example was *Felicitas*, published in 1909 by Cundy Bettoney, which had long been used in manuscript by Hall's Orchestra. Some were pieces that had been played in manuscript, but never presented to the publisher (for example *The Commander*, dedicated to Hall's pupil, F. Louise Horne). Others were isolated strains that the music arrangers at the publishing firms Cundy Bettoney and Ernest S. Williams assembled into likely marches. These, though playable, contained elements that were inconsistent with Hall's established style and were probably added or altered at the time of publication. An example is the extended trio in *North Easton*.

Some of these included parts of marches that had previously been published, or even were published in their entirety while Hall was still living. For example, *Old Guard*, published in 1914 by Cundy Bettoney, contained the first strain of *Trinity Bells*, which had been published in 1904 by Lyon and Healy, and was dedicated to Hall's sister, Alice.

The "rain barrel" marches, then, are a mixed bag in terms of quality and authenticity. The material is all Hall, though some of it rejected material; the assembly was left up to the publishing houses. They provided Isabella with income, and they served to keep Hall's name before the public with new releases for eight years after his death.

One of these marches, *The Imperial Life Guards March*, was brought out in 1908 by John Church, who had previously published many of Hall's marches. This was the seventeenth, and enabled Church to put out a book of 16 marches, the "R. B. Hall Superior Band Book," omitting *The Charge of the Battalion* (1898) which was far more difficult than the other Church marches. Since band books were a very popular format, this book enjoyed wide distribution, and boosted Hall's reputation significantly.

Between 1908 and 1915 fifteen Hall pieces were published: thirteen marches; a schottische; and a ragtime two-step, *A Georgia Jade*. Of these, about half appear to be as Hall wrote them, and about half appear to be assembled from parts, or reconstructed.

North Easton March, by R. B. Hall. Solo Cornet part.[1]

The marches published in 1908 were mostly works Hall had completed but not published. *Adalid* was one of the original "R.C.B." (Richmond Cornet Band) marches from the 1870's. *Commander* was an interesting case where the dedication was preserved although the title was changed from the one Hall had originally given it. As published in 1908 by Ernest S. Williams, *Commander* carries the dedicatory line "Dedicated to Miss

F. Louise Horne" above the title on the solo cornet part.

The manuscript score for this same music also bears the dedication in a short form: "To F. Louise Horne." The title of the manuscript, however, is "Imperial Guard's," written in Hall's hand, together with his familiar signature. We can therefore be sure that this is the music that Hall wanted to go with the dedication, even though the title was changed.

Despite the confusing title on the score of *Commander*, the music is not what Church published in 1908 as *The Imperial Life Guards March*. The latter is an entirely different march which is typical of Hall's very late style. *The Imperial Life Guards March* is thematically related throughout, and in the quadrille style with which Hall was experimenting in his last years. (cf. *Exalted Ruler*, and *Cavalier*.) It appears that the title and the content of the two marches was swapped or switched by the publishers.

Also in 1908 came *The Ensign*, which has been said to have been one of the early "R.C.B." marches: in style it might be, except for the stinger which could have been added. *Eternal Rest*, a funeral march, appears to be original. It was affirmed as original by oral sources James Varney and Arthur Roundy who remembered playing it while Hall was alive. *Ino*, a "Barn Dance Schottische" was published for small orchestra; the earlier manuscript score, for small band, bears the title "Everlina" in Hall's hand, but other than being transposed up a step, the music is essentially unchanged. It is a typical Hall march in form, with contrasting first strain, second strain, and trio sections, and appropriate introductions. It differs in that it captures the schottische rhythm (dotted eighths and sixteenths) and is in four/four time rather than alla-breve as a march would be in order to provide for a smoothly danceable tempo. I arranged this piece for modern band instrumentation in 1986, and it has been performed by the Bangor Band on numerous occasions since then.[2]

In 1909, two years after Hall's death, publisher Ernest Williams brought out *A Georgia Jade*, a ragtime two-step. Similar in style to the earlier *Creole Queen*, this also appears to be something Hall had in the works at the time of his final illness. Nothing further was published until in 1911 Star Music Company brought out *Quaboag*, named after a resort lake in northern Massachusetts. This march is an exact duplication of the 1896 *March 6/8*. Only the title and publisher have been changed.

In 1912, on February 14, Hall's widow married Samuel Philbrook of Lynn, Massachusetts. Thereafter her copyright renewals read Isabella Hall-Philbrook, which led some to speculate that she had married the eponymous Col. Philbrook of R. B. Hall's 1895 march. Further investigation indicates there was no relation.[3]

Two years later, in 1914, most of the remaining "rain barrel" marches were published, they were: *Androscoggin*; *Angelica*, which had previously been published by Ramsdell in 1891; *North Easton*, named for a town in northern Massachusetts; *Old Guard*, which truly is made of bits and pieces, including some of *Trinity Bells* and *Felicitas*; and, finally, *Resilient*, which was *The Ensign*, renamed with a trio extension added.

Last to be published was *Pine Tree State*, brought out by Cundy Bettoney in 1915. Two years later, in 1917, Carl Fischer published an orchestra edition of the "R.B.H. Book of World Famous Marches," arranged for full orchestra. This was accomplished by transposing the marches up or down a step or half-step to facilitate playing by strings.[4]

Between 1917 and 1921 Mace Gay's copyrights on the Hall marches in his collection were up for renewal, and he obtained renewals on all of them, eventually selling them in 1934 to the Walter Jacobs company. Gay had owned many Hall marches outright, that is without royalty agreements, and they had done very well for him. Mace Gay died in 1936.

Jacobs published the collection under the title *R. B. Hall's Band Book of his Most Famous Marches*, and had good success with it. In spite of that he soon sold the rights and the plates to Waterloo Music Company, in Ontario Canada. Here they were reprinted, sold as the *Waterloo Book of Hall's Marches,* and widely distributed well into the 1950's. It should be noted that both Jacobs and Waterloo deleted all of the dedications and all of the original copyright dates from the march plates. That meant that this material was not available to the players who were interested in Hall, and is one reason why there was so much curiosity about the quaint early titles. They obviously meant something, but what?

Beginning in 1921, Carl Fischer's copyrights began to be up for renewal. Because of the royalty agreements, these copyrights were renewed by Hall's widow, which is why the Fischer book we know today bears the name of Isabella Hall-Philbrook as the last copyright holder. John Church Company did not seek to renew the copyrights on their Hall marches, and they passed into the public domain between 1931 and 1943.

Many of the remaining "rain barrel" manuscripts were collected in the early 1960's by Ralph Gould. He eventually donated them to the Maine State Archives, from which they were removed to the Bagaduce Music Lending Library, in Blue Hill, Maine. They

may be viewed there, but not borrowed. Included are manuscript scores for fragments of Hall's uncompleted opera "May Blossoms," or as he titled it "Mignonette," as well as some very early religious songs, a negro dialect plantation song, and other juvenilia. Also available there are scores to *Felicitas, Commander* under the title *Imperial Guard's*[sic], and two other marches, one of which is an early sketch of *Adalid*, with some phrases precisely like the finished version, some phrases similar, and some entirely different. There is also a six-eight march unlike any of the published marches, and several sketches in an immature version of Hall's hand that provides a glimpse into his formative struggles, before his manuscript assumed the swift, practiced legibility of his mature style.

THE LOST TITLES AND THE "R.C.B." MARCHES

Hall fanciers over the years have spent considerable time and energy trying to track down some titles which were said to have been written by Hall, but have never been located or heard. First among these is *Cherryfield* for the Cherryfield Band, followed by *Garland*, for the Garland band, and *Winslow*, for the Winslow band. All these were bands that Hall taught at some time during his career as an itinerant or peripatetic band leader. Were they ever really written?

Although some of Hall's pieces, especially his later marches, have so much thematic interrelationship between strains that they had to have been conceived as a single composition from beginning to end, this is not the case with all of Hall's works. Hall had long had the habit of working on marches strain by strain, and then assembling them. This was especially true during his earlier years, when he was traveling by train from place to place to give band rehearsals. Cherryfield, Maine, band leader Charlie Wakefield told of this work style in connection with Bardwell's questioning about the rumored march entitled *Cherryfield*:

> *Well, he'd compose a first strain, a second strain, and trios by the dozens, you know. Carried 'em round in his pockets. And he matches up trios that he thought would go well, you know. Like "Greeting to Bangor," and those old standards.*[5]

The march *Cherryfield*, although many band players had spoken of its existence, was never discovered, because although Hall had called it *Cherryfield* while in Cherryfield, he called it something else when rehearsing it elsewhere. Wakefield tells Bardwell of this aspect of Hall's style:

> *And I told him about R. B. Hall writing first strains, and second strains and trios. And having them in his pocket, and every*

time he had some time off he'd sit down and dash off a strain, you know. And dedicate it to someone, wherever he happened to be.

And there was one fellow in this town by the name of Eaton. Name was Charles Eaton, E-A-T-O-N and he and R. B. Hall were bosom pals.

While Hall was down, just to show his facility, while Hall was down here, he composed a march and called it "Eaton's March" but that, too, became merged with some other march, I don't know the history. Hall would make a strain, make a march, put together, and have a name for it. Then for some unknown reason he'd change the name for something else. So again there was a march "Cherryfield," and there was an "Eaton's March," that my father had mentioned to me, but they became parts of other marches, and lost as far as name is concerned.[6]

Wakefield's comment that the pieces were "lost as far as name is concerned" is the key to the search for some of Hall's "missing" titles. It is not that *Cherryfield* was never written, it is that it was never considered permanent. When it suited Hall's convenience the title became something else or the strains were combined differently. This explains why Bardwell was to search in vain for

Garland, *Winslow*, and similar titles mentioned by old-time Hall followers, but never actually found. It also explains titles found in Hall's manuscript that were published as something else, for example *The Comical Indian*, which was published as *Algerine*. That is also the key to the *R.C.B.* marches number *1,2,* and *3*. Two of them became *Adalid* and *Adjutant Bridge*. The fate of the third has been speculated upon by bandsmen for years. It may have become *The Ensign*, or it may have never become anything at all, and be the untitled and unpublished manuscript for an early style 6/8 march that is still with the juvenile manuscripts.

NOTES

[1] R. B. Hall, *North Easton*, (Boston, Massachusetts: Cundy Bettony, 1914).

[2] The manuscript score can be seen in the Bagaduce Music Lending Library, Blue Hill, Maine. The published small orchestra parts and piano score can be seen in the Thomas C. Bardwell collection at the Special Collections, Fogler Library, University of Maine, Orono, Maine. My arrangement for modern band is in the Bangor Band Library, 647 Main Street, Bangor Maine.

[3] A discussion of this point is found in Chapter Eleven.

[4] Because of the way stringed instruments are tuned players find it easier to finger notes in keys having sharps than in keys having flats. The opposite is true for brass instruments. Therefore a march written in the key of F for band would sound better in G for orchestra; likewise a piece in A-flat for band might go better in A for orchestra.

[5] NA#2261.066.

[6] NA#2261.072-73.

CHAPTER ELEVEN
MEMORIALS TO HALL

It is precisely because Hall's marches speak for themselves as a permanent testimonial to his musicality that he is regarded as one of Maine's most important musical geniuses. The general public, however, does not often recognize or remember musical greatness without the trappings of show business and public display. Because a devoted following of band musicians, together with local history enthusiasts, has had a special fondness for Hall's legacy, on various occasions since Hall's death there have been several attempts to memorialize him in a visible and public way.

Luther C. Bateman's feature article in the Lewiston Journal Magazine Section of July 15, 1922, was approximately concurrent with the fifteenth anniversary of Hall's death.[1] This was also about the time when Hall's widow renewed the copyrights on his Carl Fischer publications.

In 1936, a bandstand was erected in Waterville's Averill Park through the efforts of a group headed up by Mr. Harry T. Drew, leader of Drew's Waterville Band. (See photo, next page). It was dedicated as the "R. B. Hall Memorial" on August 14, 1936, in a public ceremony complete with a fine souvenir program and an appearance by Hall's widow, Mrs. Isabella Hall-Philbrook. One copy of the program remains on display at the Waterville Historical Society's Redington Museum on Silver street in Waterville; another is part of the R. B. Hall Anthology, now in the Thomas C. Bardwell collection at Fogler Library, University of Maine.

At the time of this dedication, R. B. Hall's gold-plated Boston Three Star "Ne Plus Ultra" cornet, which had been given to the Waterville Historical Society by Hall's widow, was played one final time by the young Waterville cornet soloist, Earl Glazier. Then it was permanently installed in a display case at the Redington Museum, where it may be seen to this day. The bandstand, made of wood and already rotting away for lack of paint and repair, was destroyed by fire just twelve years after its dedication.

PLATE 14. R. B. HALL MEMORIAL BAND STAND 1936 (Courtesy of Bagaduce Music Lending Library)

At about this same time, Mrs. Hall-Philbrook donated a set of band instruments to the Richmond elementary school in hopes of forming a school band to rejuvenate the by-then-defunct town band in Richmond. The school, however had no program or facility for band instruction, although one of the teachers took on the duty of trying to start a band. After some initial interest, the instruments were soon unusable for lack of repairs and maintenance. Some were appropriated by students and passed out of inventory. Others simply gathered dust in the school basement, where a few unplayable battered hulks of baritone horns remain to this day.

At the thirty-fifth anniversary of Hall's death (1952) Mildred Beedle Fossett and Beth Haines (daughter of William D. Haines who led the Waterville Military Band from 1905 until 1926) each published the lengthy journalistic pieces memorializing Hall that have been quoted and cited so extensively elsewhere in this paper. The Waterville sesquicentennial of the same year brought Hall's name to the forefront once again in conjunction with the celebration of Waterville's history. A short article by Colby's long time music department chairman Dr. Ermanno F. Comparetti credited Hall with making Waterville the home of a "long series of excellent bands."[2]

A short period of neglect ensued, broken in 1958 by the *Portland Sunday Telegram*'s feature including Dr. Fred Maxwell's recollections of Hall in Bangor.[3] Next, a memorial concert by Chandler's band in Portland, on Sunday, July 10, 1960, was accompanied by a newspaper story that contained more misinformation concerning Hall than it did correct information.[4] Among the gaffes included in this short piece was that of calling the composer "Robert Bruce Hall," a mistake that was perpetuated by the United States Marine Band library, which to this day lists Hall's works under that mistaken name.

The resurgence of interest in Hall's life has been led more recently by Ralph Gould and Clinton Graffam, who worked to promote recognition for Hall during in the 1960's. Gould was a businessman with a strong avocational interest in music, whose activities included personal participation in music making, management of music organizations such as the Portland Symphony Orchstra and the Maine Music Camp, and a long list of philanthropies in music education.[5] Graffam, widely recognized for his work as a music educator, was for many years director of the band at South Portland's Deering High School, where he developed and maintained an exemplary band and orchestra.

In 1964, Gould financed, and Graffam recorded with the Deering High School band, a long-playing record of the fifteen marches in the *R. B. H. Band Book* published by Carl Fischer. The original pressings were quickly sold and distributed, and are no longer available.[6]

A Colby College testimonial concert in 1960 was given as a "Tribute to Hall."[7] Four years later famed conductor and clinician Harold B. Bachman offered his own tribute

program for Hall.[8]   Shortly thereafter, the R.B. Hall Memorial Band was begun in Waterville, a movement led by band manager Ed Pinkham, and director Brian Hutchinson.

At the same time, but on a national level, Thomas C. Bardwell, Sr., was working on the "R. B. Hall Memorial Anthology" of band tape recordings. Both his recording workshop and the collection were kept in a cottage next to his home on Martha's Vineyard Island, Massachusetts.   Bardwell conducted extensive research into Hall's biography and music from sources outside Maine, as well as traveling to Maine and interviewing extensively during research trips to Richmond, Waterville, and other scenes of Hall's activity. Bardwell published articles on Hall, as did Gould.   Each of these men interviewed the last living students of Hall in Waterville, Arthur F. Roundy, and James Varney.

In 1967, a ceremony was held at Evergreen Cemetery, marking the 60th anniversary of Hall's death. The Bath Band played, and Roundy and Varney placed a wreath on Hall's grave.

Working with band recording enthusiast and philanthropist Robert Hoe, Jr., Bardwell obtained fine recordings of the marches from the "Hall's Superior," (John Church,) and "Mace Gay" (Jacobs-Waterloo) collections made by the

PLATE 15. ARTHUR F. ROUNDY AND JAMES A. VARNEY Decorating Hall's Grave June, 1967 (Courtesy of Raymond Fogler Library Special Collections)

United States Coast Guard Band. Hoe had previously included several Hall marches from the Fischer book, in performance by the United States Navy Band, in the first volume of his extensive series of "Heritage of the March" recordings.[9] Together with Bardwell's own tapings of the Coast Guard Band, these Hall recordings formed the genesis of Bardwell's *R. B. Hall Anthology*.

In addition to his work with the *Anthology*, Bardwell felt that the State of Maine should make a visible memorial to Hall in the form of a bridge, a portion of the interstate highway, or some other large and noticeable structure that would be seen by Maine's residents and its many visitors.[10] Efforts for that sort of a memorial have not met with success, primarily because musicians who want to see Hall memorialized have been able to attract relatively little political support.

In 1978, an effort was begun to have a postage stamp commemorating R. B. Hall issued by the United States Postal service. Edward Pinkham, a prime mover in the R. B. Hall Memorial Band, was a postal employee in Waterville. Together with Bardwell and University of New Hampshire Professor Robert Swift, Pinkham managed to generate some enthusiasm, but not enough to get the stamp issued despite an active effort that continued well into 1982. Supporters of the proposal included then United States Postmaster

General William F. Bolger and United States Senator Edward Kennedy.[11] Eventually the Citizens' Stamp Advisory Committee, working on a national level, eliminated Hall's name from the list of proposals in 1983.

This effort enlisted the aid of Robert Hudson, at that time director of music at University of Maine in Augusta, and also of the Augusta (civic) Symphony and its associated Augusta Symphony Band. This alliance produced the discussions that started the campaign to get the last Saturday in June declared "R. B. Hall Day." The idea for R. B. Hall Day was originally Hudson's and the majority of the work in getting it passed in the legislature was due to his sustained effort, and to his presence in Augusta, the State capital.

Following a lengthy process of letter writing, legislative lobbying, and other political machinations, the Maine State Legislature passed a bill which was signed on May 11, 1981, by Governor Joseph Brennan, establishing the last Saturday of each June as the official observance of an annual "R. B. Hall Day." The governor issued a proclamation according to the terms of the act, which requires that "the Governor shall annually issue a proclamation inviting and urging the people of the state to observe the day with appropriate ceremony and activity."[12] The first annual R. B. Hall Day was held on Saturday, June 27, 1981 on Gardiner

APPROVED

MAY 11 '81

BY GOVERNOR

STATE OF MAINE

IN THE YEAR OF OUR LORD NINETEEN HUNDRED AND EIGHTY-ONE

H. P. 1093 — L. D. 1290

AN ACT to Establish an R. B. Hall Day to Honor and Commemorate a Great Maine Composer.

Emergency preamble. Whereas, Acts of the Legislature do not become effective until 90 days after adjournment unless enacted as emergencies; and

Whereas, the purpose of this bill is to dedicate the last Saturday in June in commemoration of R. B. Hall, a great Maine composer; and

Whereas, the last Saturday in June of this year will pass before the normal effective date of this Act; and

Whereas, in the judgment of the Legislature, these facts create an emergency within the meaning of the Constitution of Maine and required the following legislation as immediately necessary for the preservation of the public peace, health and safety; now, therefore,

Be it enacted by the People of the State of Maine, as follows:

1 MRSA § 119 is enacted to read:

§ 119. R. B. Hall Day

The last Saturday in June of each year shall be designated R. B. Hall Day and the Governor shall annually issue a proclamation inviting and urging the people of the State to observe the day with appropriate ceremony and activity. R. B. Hall Day shall commemorate and honor R. B. Hall, an internationally recognized composer. Recognized primarily as a composer of marches, he was an accomplished conductor and cornet soloist, whose creative talent and native ability marked him as one of Maine's outstanding citizens.

Emergency clause. In view of the emergency cited in the preamble, this Act shall take effect when approved.

L.D. 1290, An Act to Establish R.B. Hall Day. Approved by the Governor of the State of Maine in May, 1981.

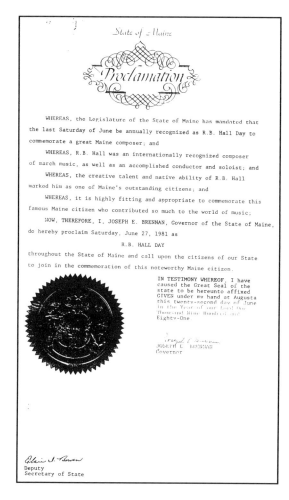

Proclamation signed by Maine Governor Joseph E. Brennan, declaring the last Saturday in June each year to be R. B. Hall Day. The first R. B. Hall Day was June 27, 1981.

Common with ten bands present. It was followed by an old-time social with the Augusta Symphony Ragtime Ensemble in the evening.

A fitting and perpetual tribute, R. B. Hall Day has been observed every year since then. A different community band hosts the festivities each year, and an ever increasing number of bands from around the state come to participate in the day-long festivals. The opportunity for the bands to hear each other is the greatest since the days of the Lake Maranacook band contests of a century ago, and the musical effort and diversity in programming have improved steadily over the past twelve years. Each band programs at least one Hall march, and some of the bands perform several. The Bangor Band has taken the occasion to program many of the less readily available and therefore less often heard Hall pieces.

What could be a more appropriate memorial to the man who wrote so many marches, taught so many bands, inspired so many players, and did so much for music in the State of Maine, than to honor his memory in this way?

Hall is remembered nationally and internationally for his genius in march writing. His many marches are still played by bands the world over. In Maine, he is remembered as "Maine's March King." He was a local musician who achieved national fame with his music. Hall differed from many other bandmaster-composers of his era, primarily because his compositions were so well-crafted. His mastery of the subtleties of the march form was so complete that his works achieved an enduring popularity for the composer, and a place for him in the hearts of band musicians everywhere.

NOTES

[1] Luther C. Bateman, "Maine's March King - Richmond Musician's Music Enjoyed By Royalty," *Lewiston* [Maine] *Journal*, 15 July 1922, M1-2.

[2] Ermanno F. Comparetti, "Waterville's Musical Horizons Expanding", *Waterville* [Maine] *Morning Sentinel*, 3 March 1954, 3.

[3] John Fuller, "Hall Composed Music To Beat The Band," *Portland* [Maine] *Sunday Telegram*, 26 October 1958, 1D. (Hereafter, *PST*).

[4] *PST*, 10 July 1960, 7A.

[5] An interview with Ralph Gould that embraces many of these topics is found in NA#2262.

[6] Although no copies of the original recording are available, several band directors have kept taped copies. The cover (with no recording in it) including notes by Gould and Graffam can be seen at the Bagaduce Music Lending Library, Blue Hill, Maine, as part of the Hall collection. Bardwell also transcribed this record onto tape; in this form it is part of the "R. B. Hall Anthology" and can be heard at the Listening Center, Fogler Library, University of Maine, Orono, Maine.

[7] The program for this concert can be seen in the Hall colection at the Bagaduce Music Lending Library, Blue Hill, Maine. The concert was given on April 7-9, 1960 at the Waterville Opera House. A short write-up on Hall was included, but only two of his marches were played.

[8] The program for this concert can be seen in the Hall collection at the Bagaduce Music Lending Library, Blue Hill, Maine. The concert was given on June 24, 1964, at Hauck Auditorium, University of Maine, Orono, Maine.

[9] Robert Hoe, Jr., ed., *Heritage of the March*, vols. 1, C, E, H, P, T, MM, OO, WW.

[10] Bardwell, *Music Journal Anthology*, (1968), 102.

_____, *Fanfare*, (1977), 30.

NA#2228.024.

[11] Letter from Bolger to Kennedy, 11 December 1978.

[12] H. P. 1093—L. D. 1290, 11 May 1981: Maine Public Law ch. 246, art. 119.

INDEX

A

A Georgia Jade two-step: 46, 122, 123
Adalid march: 122, 124, 125
Adjutant Bridge march: 19, 24, 34, 125
Albania Orchestra: 68
Albanian march: 65, 72
Albany: 61, 65-72, 75, 82, 97
Algerine: 34, 125
American Belle march: 89
American Cadet Band: 34, 78, 80, 81, 118
American Cadet march: 50
 similarity to The High School Cadets: 51
Andrews' Orchestra: 9, 11-15, 25, 30, 31, 34, 97, 102
Androscoggin march: 123
Angelica march: 123
Appleton march: 52

B

Bangor Band: 11-12, 14, 15-20, 23-31, 52,
    55, 97, 118, 119, 131
Bangor march: 34
Barcelona Bolero for cornet: 49
Browne Family Orchestra: 2, 3

C

Canabas Club: 40, 101, 104, 116
Canabas march: 104
Canton Halifax march: 48
Carl Fischer: 50, 51, 58, 65, 84, 97,
    116, 123, 124, 127, 129

Cavalier march: 123
Chandler's Band: 34, 128
Chandler's march: 34
Chapman, William Rogers: 86, 87, 89
Charge of the Battalion march: 89
Cherryfield march: 124
Chilcothian march: 34
Col. Brett march: 34
Col. Fitch march: 65, 72
Col. Perkins march: 34
Col. Philbrook march: 84
Colby: 83, 96, 98, 101, 102, 103, 128, 129
Commonwealth march: 87, 94
Creole Queen cakewalk: 46, 123
Cundy Bettoney: 121, 123

D

Dallas march: 52
De Molay Commandery march: 49
Dinsmore's Orchestra: 37, 40, 43, 48, 56, 104
Dunlap Commandery march: 53, 94

E

E-flat to B-flat cornet: 4-5
Elgie, Augustus: 68, 69
Eternal Rest march: 123
Everlina: 123
Exalted Ruler march: 107, 123

INDEX, CONT.

INDEX, CONT.

INDEX, CONT.